CHRISTMAS AND THE REAL WORLD

SCENES OF HARDSHIP, GRACE, AND PEACE

HOWARD LAWLER

Christmas and the Real World: Scenes of Hardship, Grace, and Peace

ISBN: 979-8-218-09832-2

Salpizo Publications
Wake Forest, NC

For my sister Carol—a far greater gift to me than all the Christmas presents I ever received combined.

"I should count a life well spent, and the world well lost, if, after tasting all its experiences and facing all its problems, I had no more to show at its close, or to carry with me to another life, than the acquisition of a real, sure, humble, and grateful faith in the Eternal and Incarnate Son of God."

P. T. Forsyth

CONTENTS

SEEING BEYOND SANTA

"For we do not have a high priest who is unable to sympathize with our weaknesses, but one who has been tempted in every way as we are, yet without sin. Therefore, let us approach the throne of grace with boldness, so that we may receive mercy and find grace to help us in time of need."
Hebrews 4:15-16

It was the Xbox of my primitive youth. Now it seems like Jurassic technology but it wowed me then. Even in the present techno-age people still buy it. The humble View-Master seems here to stay.

I had many of the reels (14 photos each rendering 7 scenes in 3-D) including Roy Rogers, Hansel and Gretel, and Alice in Wonderland. The scenes carried me near and far. I toured the United Nations building and then anticipated the landing on the moon. I lingered over Niagara Falls frozen almost solid or bathed in color at night. I gazed down at Tarzan swinging through the forest. I gawked at dinosaurs scrambling from a fissure that belched volcanic rubble into a ruby sky. I spied Santa on a snow-clad roof.

I invite you to view my book as a virtual View-Master reel that offers scenes of Christmas. View-Master gives seven photos per reel. I will offer eight. My old reels ran the gamut from pure fantasy (Goldilocks) to harsh reality (The War Between the States). This book is about reality.

American culture tends to push Christmas into the fantasy camp. I do not mind a bit of myth and mirth. During my childhood, a plaster sculpture of Santa snoozing in an overstuffed chair formed part of our holiday decorations. Perhaps he suffered sugar shock. I inherited the heirloom and display it every December.

My Santa figure has friends. Snowmen, Elf on the Shelf, and Yukon Cornelius keep him company. I like Rudolph's funny nose. I am glad bumbles bounce and that the North Pole now has dental care. Christmas lights, tinsel, and turkey are right up my alley. I like fake snow and the real thing too, but I know that it takes much more than yule trimmings to fortify us for life. The real world demands more than holiday diversions.

We have more—much, much more. We have Jesus. Buy a View-Master if you like, but make sure you pursue a healthy view of the Master.

Seasonal knickknacks return to plastic tubs to sleep away the other seasons. Jesus never slumbers. He rules. He must guide our choices, not the holiday tchotchkes.

We must follow him when the tree lights are in back storage and we walk through the valley of the shadow of death.

Christmas is for the real world. We need to know that in tough times. Life holds plenty of those seasons and we rarely see them coming:

- You grow weary from the daily grind.
- You lose a job you loved.
- Finances are tight.
- The government burdens you with onerous taxes.
- People insult you.
- Your spouse mistrusts you.
- Your family is distant.
- A friend betrays you.
- You are forced to relocate.
- You struggle with depression.
- Loneliness haunts your nights.
- Ministry has drained you dry.
- You feel like a failure.
- You are becoming aware of the true depth of your sin.

I have experienced much of that list. I have also wrestled with hardships that are not on that list.

Frosty the Snowman cannot help you bear such burdens. Jesus can. He came to face the real world. He faced terrible pressure in all aspects of life yet never failed. He offers unparalleled hope throughout hardships. Most of all, he offers his grace in the face of our sin and guilt.

The meditations in this book explore the realism of Christmas revealed in the Bible. We will ponder how the Christmas story and other passages connect with our lives. A song will finish each meditation. I offer these reflections on hardship and hope to encourage you. I want you to enjoy them. Whatever you face, please employ them.

O come, O come, Emmanuel,
And ransom captive Israel,
That mourns in lonely exile here,
Until the Son of God appear.
Rejoice! Rejoice! Emmanuel
Shall come to thee, O Israel.

O come, Thou Dayspring, come and cheer,
Our spirits by Thine advent here;
Disperse the gloomy clouds of night,
And death's dark shadows put to flight.
Rejoice! Rejoice! Emmanuel
Shall come to thee, O Israel.

O come, Thou Wisdom from on high,
And order all things, far and nigh;
To us the path of knowledge show,
And cause us in her ways to go.
Rejoice! Rejoice! Emmanuel
Shall come to thee, O Israel.

O come, Desire of nations, bind,
All peoples in one heart and mind;

Bid envy, strife and quarrels cease,
Fill all the world with heaven's peace.
Rejoice! Rejoice! Emmanuel
Shall come to thee, O Israel.[1]

THE HOPES AND FEARS
OF ALL THE YEARS

*"Hope delayed makes the heart sick,
but desire fulfilled is a tree of life."*
Proverbs 13:12

A flurry of television specials tells our culture when the Christmas season is upon us. Frosty, Rudolph, Kris Kringle, cooking shows, concerts, and tree lightings provide pleasant stuff separated from unpleasant realities. Nobody in fantasyland wears an N95 mask—not even on the Island of Misfit Toys. Christmas and calamity quarantine from each other. Saccharine here, sepsis there.

Isolating Christmas from our tough world through tinsel and trinkets is untrue to the Bible. In Scripture, Christmas and calamity stand linked. The honest display comforts us because, when all is said and done, Christmas wins.

BROADCAST CHRISTMAS—HOPES BARELY MEET FEARS

One December night I turned on the television to wind down after a long day. A figure skater glided through a holiday wonderland. The soundtrack mentioned "sin and error pining" but little indicated our planet was not as pristine as fresh snow.

Then the skating program ended. Cut to commercials. A preview of the news announced, "Children's toys stolen from the Salvation Army." Back to the real world where crooks overcome good cheer.

Our culture knows fear, fractured families, bullying, betrayal, disinformation, injustice, idolatry, poverty, greed, dirt, disease, death, and more. The biblical Christmas story features the same things. Bible-style Christmas is sober engagement rather than escapism.

Christ came to face facts, not star in a fantasy. The Bible tells us that the world fought him from the manger on. People did not delight in the arrival of the light of the world according to John 3:19-21:

> This is the judgment: The light has come into the world, and people loved darkness rather than the light because their deeds were evil. For everyone who does evil hates the light and avoids it, so that his deeds may not be exposed. But anyone who lives by the truth comes to the light, so that his works may be shown to be accomplished by God.

Human rebellion—not the earth's rotation—caused the darkness. Light-hearted holiday fare cannot dispel it. The Messiah, however, is up for the job. He did his work well indeed.

BETHLEHEM CHRISTMAS—HOPES MEET FEARS

Holiday fare tosses a problem or two into the program, but the scope is narrow and merry resolution comes quickly. The Grinch returns the stolen gifts while the "roast beast" is still fresh. The biblical account of Christmas deals with the moral mess of all centuries.

Luke 2:1-7 shows how the Roman government played a supporting role in God's redemption plan:

> In those days a decree went out from Caesar Augustus that the whole empire should be registered. This first registration took place while Quirinius was governing Syria. So everyone went to be registered, each to his own town. Joseph also went up from the town of Nazareth in Galilee, to Judea, to the city of David, which is called Bethlehem, because he was of the house and family line of David, to be registered along with Mary, who was engaged to him and was pregnant. While they were there, the time came for her to give birth. Then she gave birth to her firstborn son, and she wrapped him tightly in cloth and laid him in a manger, because there was no guest room available for them.

A money-hungry government forced a humble family to make a dangerous trip. The political machine demanded resources. Rome moved mountains and mothers to grab cash.

The Jerusalem Talmud records a rabbinic tradition that the Messiah would be born in the Royal Castle of Bethlehem. That magnificent structure crowned the highest hill southeast of town and dominated the landscape. That tradition was wrong. Isaac Watts got it right:

> No gold, nor purple swaddling bands,
> Nor royal shining things;
> A manger for his cradle stands;
> And holds the King of kings.[1]

Jesus did not get a decent guest room let alone the royal treatment. A hard world closed the door to a woman on the verge of labor.

Things became ugly after the baby arrived. Murderous lies slid from Herod's tongue. The wicked king who lived in that fine palace decreed that Bethlehem boys must die. His slaughter of children made other tongues wail in agony (Matt 2:16-18).

What is Christmas? The holiday season means fresh-baked cookies, colorful lights, Currier and Ives, sugarplums, and sleigh bells. In the Bible, we find angels and shepherds, news of great joy, gifts for a child, and peace on earth. But we see more. Christmas is also dislocation, dirt, deceit, murder, and

to them, "Do you now believe? Indeed, an hour is coming, and has come, when each of you will be scattered to his own home, and you will leave me alone. Yet I am not alone, because the Father is with me. I have told you these things so that in me you may have peace. You will have suffering in this world. Be courageous! I have conquered the world."

He conquered the world by more than his teaching. He did it in *deeds*. Consider five ways he wins.

First, he never joined the rebellion. He never sinned in thought, word, or act. His conduct always conformed to God's perfect law.

Second, he took the sins of the world on himself and dealt with them on his cross. As our substitute, he paid for all the wrong things we have done.

Third, he rose bodily from the dead. Political powers killed him but he walked out of the tomb with power over death. He will never die again.

Fourth, he did not stay even one night in Bethlehem's castle as a baby but he left Jerusalem to ascend the highest throne. The Lord's throne makes Caesar's look like a cheap folding chair.

Fifth, he will return someday and judge this world. In the end, every sin will be paid for either by Jesus for those who rely on him or by sinners who rely on themselves.

The only way we can escape paying for our sins forever is to ask Jesus to *forgive and give*—forgive our sins and give us the gift of eternal life. No good works we do can make us right with God. We cannot even help fix our sin problem. We must trust the rescue work Jesus did.

We naturally dislike the idea of condemnation for sin but we also dislike the idea of free salvation. One reason is pride. We want to earn at least part of a good standing before God. The other reason is fear. A free salvation that puts us freely at God's service unnerves us.

The salvation message always has been hard for hearers to swallow, even when the apostles first preached the gospel. Abraham Lincoln wrote, "Men are not flattered by being shown that there has been a difference of purpose between the Almighty and them."[2] Flattery can be deadly (Prov 26:28; 29:5) but the gospel gives life.

Many welcome a message that God is ready to help meet our needs as we define them. Richard John Neuhaus uses just one sentence to point to the problem: "The Christian message throws our questions into question; it challenges not so much the way we meet our needs as the way we define our needs."[3] We balk at accepting both God's definition of our needs and his humbling solution to our problem.

The message stuck in my craw for a long time. But truth is truth. Accepting the message of salvation by grace alone leads to eternal life. True life is better than any fantasy, especially the fiction we tell ourselves to avoid facing our need (Psa 36:2). Jesus alone meets the need. He does it honestly, graciously, and gloriously.

If you have never asked for the life-changing gift of salvation, do it now. Ask Jesus to forgive you and give you the gift of eternal life. I did. He did.

After leading a Christmas morning service years ago, I went home to enjoy the usual holiday customs. An hour later, I was in an inner-city morgue. A member of our church left the service and learned that a relative died. Someone had to identify the body.

From a sanctuary to a mortuary. Can Christmas make the trip? Yes.

Going from our church service to that morgue was not like switching from the saccharine festival on ice to a caustic news report. We knew that Christ was born for this. He came to a cradle and a cross to bring us eternal life. He gives hope that stands up in a decorated church and a dreary morgue. Jesus is no fable. Many people identified his resurrected body.

Knowing he lives does not make life comfortable but it conveys comfort. Jesus came so we could take our real-world worries to him and find peace. Skip broadcast Christmas if you prefer but do not miss the wonder of Jesus in Bethlehem and beyond. Hopes and fears not only met in that town but clashed. Be of good cheer. Jesus won.

O little town of Bethlehem
How still we see thee lie!
Above thy deep and dreamless sleep,
The silent stars go by.

Yet in thy dark streets shineth,
The everlasting Light;
The hopes and fears of all the years,
Are met in thee tonight.

For Christ is born of Mary,
And gathered all above,
While mortals sleep, the angels keep,
Their watch of wondering love,
O morning stars together,
Proclaim the holy birth!
And praises sing to God the King,
And Peace to men on earth.

How silently, how silently,
The wondrous gift is given!
So God imparts to human hearts,
The blessings of His heaven.
No ear may hear His coming,
But in this world of sin,
Where meek souls will receive Him still,
The dear Christ enters in.

O holy Child of Bethlehem!
Descend to us, we pray;
Cast out our sin, and enter in;

Be born in us today.
We hear the Christmas angels,
The great glad tidings tell;
O come to us, abide with us,
Our Lord Emmanuel.[4]

FRONT-PAGE NEWS

"But the angel said to them, 'Don't be afraid, for look, I proclaim to you good news of great joy that will be for all the people: Today in the city of David a Savior was born for you, who is the Messiah, the Lord.'"
Luke 2:10-11

The phrase "front-page news" reaches back to physical newspapers. Journalists in varied media still use lead stories to grab attention. Some headlines are strange—I have seen ones about belching cows, ugly dog contest winners, scorpions falling out of store garments, and spiders falling from the sky. Others are serious warnings about economic crises, pollution, pandemics, and war. Those leads shout that our world is out of order. What can anyone do to fix it?

The front page of the New Testament (as our bound Bibles are arranged) declares that one man can do the job and *has* done it. The start of the Gospel of Matthew does not seem like hot copy but it conveys news that makes a world of difference to our lives. It surveys the ancestry of Jesus and links the panorama to our problems.

THE FRONT PAGE

Editors do not put dull stories front and center. The classic example says that "Dog Bites Man" does not make the front page but "Man Bites Dog" does. Juicier still (though suspect) is "Aliens Abduct and Bite Dog." Best of all would be "Alien Dog Bites Editors for Suspect Headlines."

The genealogy that begins Matthew chapter 1 does not seem to be a hot headline candidate. It looks like "Dog Bites Man" material. Read all about it in Matthew 1:1-17:

An account of the genealogy of Jesus Christ, the Son of David, the Son of Abraham:
Abraham fathered Isaac,
Isaac fathered Jacob,
Jacob fathered Judah and his brothers,
Judah fathered Perez and Zerah by Tamar,
Perez fathered Hezron,
Hezron fathered Aram,
Aram fathered Amminadab,
Amminadab fathered Nahshon,
Nahshon fathered Salmon,
Salmon fathered Boaz by Rahab,
Boaz fathered Obed by Ruth,
Obed fathered Jesse,
and Jesse fathered King David.

David fathered Solomon by Uriah's wife,
Solomon fathered Rehoboam,
Rehoboam fathered Abijah,
Abijah fathered Asa,
Asa fathered Jehoshaphat,
Jehoshaphat fathered Joram,
Joram fathered Uzziah,
Uzziah fathered Jotham,
Jotham fathered Ahaz,
Ahaz fathered Hezekiah,
Hezekiah fathered Manasseh,
Manasseh fathered Amon,
Amon fathered Josiah,
and Josiah fathered Jeconiah and his brothers
at the time of the exile to Babylon.
After the exile to Babylon
Jeconiah fathered Shealtiel,
Shealtiel fathered Zerubbabel,
Zerubbabel fathered Abiud,
Abiud fathered Eliakim,
Eliakim fathered Azor,
Azor fathered Zadok,
Zadok fathered Achim,
Achim fathered Eliud,
Eliud fathered Eleazar,
Eleazar fathered Matthan,

Matthan fathered Jacob,
and Jacob fathered Joseph the husband of Mary,
who gave birth to Jesus who is called the Messiah.
So all the generations from Abraham to David were fourteen generations; and from David until the exile to Babylon, fourteen generations; and from the exile to Babylon until the Messiah, fourteen generations.

People often skim-read such Bible passages. Perhaps you just did.

Sales-seeking editors today would judge this genealogy as a weak lead. They need to look deeper. It holds scandals enough to satisfy any sensationalist. Most of all, it establishes that Jesus had the right background to serve as Messiah. The original Jewish audience considered that vital information. We will follow some of the twists, turns, and truths in this important record.

EXTRA, EXTRA, READ ALL ABOUT HER

Women did not appear in most genealogies of this type but here we find women. Do you know them? I assume you know Mary. Let's check the backstories of the other four.

Tamar (Gen 38) was a widow who longed for a child. When the standard approach failed to gain a husband and child, she hatched an unsavory plot. She disguised herself as a prostitute and got her immoral father-in-law, Judah, to produce a pregnancy. Tamar's deceased husband must have been spinning in his grave. Judah first denied his role but solid evidence proved his guilt. The names of Judah and the two boys Tamar bore, Perez and Zerah, appear in the genealogy. They reminded the original audience of lies, lust, and lack of faith in God.

Rahab (Josh 2, 6) was a Gentile. The first part of her name (Ra) was the name of an Egyptian god. She belonged to the idolatrous Amorite people. Inquiring minds want to know—what is a goy like her doing in a Jewish genealogy like this? A rabbi friend of mine told me about his search for a can of kosher tuna in the American south. His search ended successfully in a surprising store—the Piggly Wiggly! Putting a Gentile in a kosher genealogy is odd but there is more to the story. Tamar disguised herself to look like a prostitute but Rahab had the job. Her life changed when she saved the lives of Israelites on a reconnaissance mission. She married one of the men and joined the community of Israel. Her story ends well but would you feature an ex-prostitute in a messianic resume?

Ruth (Ruth 1-4) was an upright woman but she too was a foreigner. She belonged to the Moabite people. That tribe had a rough start. Lot's two unmarried daughters wanted children but they lived in a cave in the wild which restricted prospects for proper mates. They hatched a wicked plan and got their father rip-snorting drunk. They out-Tamar-ed Tamar. The older daughter gave birth to a son named Moab who became the patriarch of Ruth's native people.

Bathsheba (2 Sam 11-12) appears in the genealogy as "Uriah's wife." The daughter of an Israelite, she married a Hittite. Some might have counted her a foreigner because of that marriage. Her husband served David as a trustworthy military leader. The King saw her bathing, summoned her, and impregnated her. To cover his tracks, David ordered that Uriah be left vulnerable during a heated battle. Uriah's combat death was planned murder. The king tried to make people think that Uriah produced the child. David failed to fool God who sent the prophet Nathan to confront the king. David repented (see Psalm 51) but terrible consequences followed for him and many other people. If the genealogy simply used Bathsheba's name it might downplay the sordid story. The phrase "David fathered Solomon by Uriah's wife" draws attention to David's dark deed.

Why did Matthew include these four women? Why prompt memories of the unsavory acts done *by* or *to* them? Sarah had less baggage. Rebecca had almost none. I cannot answer that question, but I see a good reason for including them. The schemes and sins summoned are the stuff that made the savior come.

WHERE WE COME INTO THE STORY

The genealogy connects with today's headlines about lies, political corruption, rape, murder, and more. We properly shudder at the scandalous stories, but we can suffer a bad slip—we can forget that we are sinners, too.

Every person in that genealogy sinned against the living God. We dipped into some rancid cases but no person on that list was sinless. None could stand holy before God without his help. If we think that we are good to go because we have not done things as bad as Tamar, Lot's daughters, or King David, then we delude ourselves. All sins are serious and we have all sinned. Every sin offends God, not just the ones that make headlines.

Take a sad news report to gain perspective. A headline announced the passing of the most obese person on record. The man weighed around 1,000 pounds. I weigh far less than that. Should I conclude, therefore, that I am free from the pull of gravity? No. Though hundreds of pounds lighter than that man, I cannot leap off a skyscraper and live. We might not sin in the weighty ways that King David did against God, Bathsheba, and the nation, but our sin is still a matter of gravity. All sin pulls downward toward hell.

Sin is a grave matter. Our creator has every right to our love and obedience in every situation. Sin includes wrong attitudes and actions. Sin does more than break abstract rules; sin has broken our world. Beautiful elements remain for us to enjoy, but ugliness mars the creation. Hence the dark headlines we read while holding old-school newspapers or gazing at glowing screens. To set this world right, the sin problem must be solved.

WHERE JESUS COMES INTO THE STORY

The one true God lives eternally as Father, Son, and Holy Spirit. God the Father sent God the Son to resolve the world's sin problem and remake the world. We will unpack that truth in the next scene. For now, focus on the core fact that Jesus is true God who came here as a true human. That is what the word "incarnation" means when applied to Jesus.

The Son decided to come here to deal with our sin problem. The headline could be: "Alien Solves Sin Problem as Native." He left heavenly glory to deal with our earthly mess.

The savior reached the Bethlehem manger via the spotted lineage we read in the genealogy. Does the rot in his family tree disqualify Jesus from playing his saving role? No. The Holy Spirit worked in Mary to make the Messiah both human and pure.

The account of the divine work follows the genealogy in Matthew 1:18-25:

> The birth of Jesus Christ came about this way: After his mother Mary had been engaged to Joseph, it was discovered before they came together that she was pregnant

from the Holy Spirit. So her husband, Joseph, being a righteous man, and not wanting to disgrace her publicly, decided to divorce her secretly.

But after he had considered these things, an angel of the Lord appeared to him in a dream, saying, "Joseph, son of David, don't be afraid to take Mary as your wife, because what has been conceived in her is from the Holy Spirit. She will give birth to a son, and you are to name him Jesus, because he will save his people from their sins." Now all this took place to fulfill what was spoken by the Lord through the prophet: "See, the virgin will become pregnant and give birth to a son, and they will name him Immanuel, which is translated "God is with us."

When Joseph woke up, he did as the Lord's angel had commanded him. He married her but did not have sexual relations with her until she gave birth to a son. And he named him Jesus.

The Lord's lineage provided the right legal and regal standing. His virgin birth provided the purity his rescue mission required.

Hit pause. Someone might ask: "You do not really believe a virgin had a baby, do you? How can you write a book about the real world and include that superstitious, pre-scientific nonsense?" I do believe it and I do not regard the belief as violating science rightly conceived.

Someone might insist: "Apart from modern fertility technologies, virgins do not have babies. Mary lacked those technologies so she was not a virgin when she gave birth." I respond with questions about Major League Baseball:

- Do pitchers throw no-hitters in back-to-back starts?
- Do triple plays happen without the bat ever touching the ball?
- Do batters hit a foul ball, break a fan's nose, and then hit another foul that breaks the leg of the same fan while being carried on a stretcher?

Each event has happened once.[1] The same is true of the virgin birth.

The comeback will be: "Those baseball quirks are unlikely, yet still possible. Virgin birth as the Bible reports in Mary's case is impossible. No clear thinker doubts that." Really? Some of the best logicians in history believed in it. Many sharp thinkers still do, including scientists.

To me, the virgin birth is far more plausible than philosophical naturalism. I find it hard to believe that information-rich life forms reproduce by naturalistic means. Scientists struggle to explain how that could happen.[2]

John C. Walton, a research professor of chemistry at the University of St. Andrews, asks if "mindless nature alone" can provide the necessary information necessary for reproduction.

He fishes around in the early chemical pond imagined by some scientists and uses math as his fishing tackle. Walton notes the variables and then comes to the bottom line:

> In a prebiotic soup environment therefore, the total probability of a functional 100 unit protein forming would be 1 in 10^{63} x 10^{30} x 10^{30}, i.e. 1 in 10^{123}, and for a 150 amino acid protein this would be 1 x 10^{74} x 10^{45} x 10^{45}, i.e. 1 in 10^{164}. To form an idea of the impossibly small chance these numbers reveal, compare them with the chance of winning the national lottery jackpot, which is about 1 in 10^9, or the chance of finding one particular atom in the whole observable universe which would be 'only' 1 in 10^{80}.[3]

To write that number fully you need 164 zeros following the number 10. Every zero multiplies the preceding number 10 times. The odds apply to forming just one protein! The staggering information load points to a mind and a mastermind.

The virgin birth is logical if you use the correct premises: the creator exists and acts in history. God made the universe out of nothing and God can make a baby without the help of a human father and any sexual relations. In Luke's account of the virgin birth, the angel Gabriel tells Mary in Luke 1:37: "For nothing will be impossible with God." Reasonable enough.

I believe in the virgin birth because the Bible teaches it. I have confidence in the Bible because I have confidence in Jesus.

It seems wise to side with the most influential human in history.

The God of galaxies can make a virgin birth. He can handle any problem we face. Whether we realize it or not, sin is our problem of first importance.

THE GOOD NEWS

God solved our worst problem through the best human. Jesus is one of us but, unlike all of us, he never sinned. We all have sinned. Jesus was born, died, rose, and reigns to save *us* from *us*. He gives the gift of eternal life to those who rely on him alone.

The Lord's grateful servant Paul reports the life-giving and life-changing news in Ephesians 2:1-13:

> And you were dead in your trespasses and sins in which you previously walked according to the ways of this world, according to the ruler of the power of the air, the spirit now working in the disobedient. We too all previously lived among them in our fleshly desires, carrying out the inclinations of our flesh and thoughts, and we were by nature children under wrath as the others were also. But God, who is rich in mercy, because of his great love that he had for us, made us alive with Christ even though we were dead in trespasses. You are saved by grace! He also raised us up with him and seated us with him in the heavens in Christ Jesus,

so that in the coming ages he might display the immeasurable riches of his grace through his kindness to us in Christ Jesus. For you are saved by grace through faith, and this is not from yourselves; it is God's gift—not from works, so that no one can boast. For we are his workmanship, created in Christ Jesus for good works, which God prepared ahead of time for us to do. So, then, remember that at one time you were Gentiles in the flesh—called "the uncircumcised" by those called "the circumcised," which is done in the flesh by human hands. At that time you were without Christ, excluded from the citizenship of Israel, and foreigners to the covenants of promise, without hope and without God in the world. But now in Christ Jesus, you who were far away have been brought near by the blood of Christ.

The Lord's cross dealt decisively with the breadth and depth of sin. He did it for Jewish people like Matthew and Gentiles like me. No one else has the right qualifications and power to do the job.

On the cross, the only sinless human paid the penalty we earned. He died exhausting the just sentence we would have served in hell. He rose bodily from the dead to show he is all-powerful. King David dealt death to Uriah and then died. King Jesus died and he gives life to all kinds of people.

I am one of his rescued sinners. Are you? If not, why not become one now? Quietly call on him from your heart for the gift.

Turn to him for life. Do not turn over a new leaf and try to be better. Trust the savior to apply his perfect human record to you. God the judge sees savior-reliant people as possessing the Lord's righteous resume. God the Holy Spirit will work in you to change your life for God's glory. In the end, Jesus will take you to resurrection glory.

We read about the Lord's ancestors on the front page of the New Testament and find people we would not have included. Jesus saw people who need him. He came for their sakes and ours. Nellie Simmons-Randall wrote a poem entitled "If You Could See Your Ancestors" which poses probing questions:

If you could see your ancestors
All standing in a row,
Would you be proud of them or not?
Or don't you really know?

Some strange discoveries are made
In climbing family trees.
And some of them, you know,
Do not particularly please.

If you could see your ancestors
All standing in a row,
There might be some of them perhaps
You shouldn't care to know.

But here's another question
Which requires a different view
If you could "meet" your ancestors
Would they be proud of you?[4]

Her final question is interesting but not crucial. The key issue is how we see Jesus. In 1 Corinthians 1:28-31, Paul calls the church family to take pride in Jesus alone:

God has chosen what is insignificant and despised in the world—what is viewed as nothing—to bring to nothing what is viewed as something, so that no one may boast in his presence. It is from him that you are in Christ Jesus, who became wisdom from God for us—our righteousness, sanctification, and redemption—in order that, as it is written: "Let the one who boasts, boast in the Lord."

Boast in the Lord who was born miraculously in Bethlehem. Boast in the Lord who died, rose, and reigns. Jesus is the best news any sinner ever heard or ever will.

Come, Thou long-expected Jesus,
Born to set Thy people free;
From our fears and sins release us;
Let us find our rest in Thee.
Israel's strength and consolation,

Hope of all the earth Thou art,
Dear Desire of every nation,
Joy of every longing heart.

Born Thy people to deliver,
Born a Child, and yet a King,
Born to reign in us forever,
Now Thy gracious kingdom bring.
By Thine own eternal Spirit,
Rule in all our hearts alone;
By Thine all-sufficient merit,
Raise us to Thy glorious throne.[5]

LOWER THAN ANGELS CAN GO

"Who is like the LORD our God—
the one enthroned on high,
who stoops down to look
on the heavens and the earth?"
Psalm 113:5-6

"You are the man I have been dreaming of." Eve Arden said that line to Groucho Marx in the movie "At the Circus." Groucho replied with a question: "What do you eat before you go to bed?"[1]

Do you ever have bizarre dreams? Nighttime noshing accounts for some curious reveries. Many are meaningless.

Almost 2,000 years before Christ came, the patriarch Jacob had a strange but meaningful dream. Genesis 28:12 says what he saw: "A stairway was set on the ground with its top reaching the sky, and God's angels were going up and down on it." Jacob's diet did not over-rev his REM sleep. God expanded Jacob's vision.

Jacob's stairway lifts our spiritual gaze, pointing to a place more exalted than the one we inhabit. Angels can descend from that domain to ours. We see that in the Christmas story. Angels came to predict, announce, and celebrate Christ's birth.

The main descent story, however, does not concern angels. God the Son descended to do the work of God on earth. When Jesus descended that first Christmas, he went lower than angels can go.

Philippians 2:1-11 explains the point of Christmas. The Apostle Paul tells the church how far Christ went and why he made the trip:

> If, then, there is any encouragement in Christ, if any consolation of love, if any fellowship with the Spirit, if any affection and mercy, make my joy complete by thinking the same way, having the same love, united in spirit, intent on one purpose. Do nothing out of selfish ambition or conceit, but in humility consider others as more important than yourselves. Everyone should look not to his own interests, but rather to the interests of others. Adopt the same attitude as that of Christ Jesus, who, existing in the form of God, did not consider equality with God as something to be exploited. Instead he emptied himself by assuming the form of a servant, taking on the likeness of humanity. And when he had come as a man, he humbled himself by becoming obedient to the point of death—even to death on a cross. For this reason God highly exalted him and gave him the name that is above every name, so that at the name of Jesus every knee will bow—in

heaven and on earth and under the earth—and every tongue will confess that Jesus Christ is Lord, to the glory of God the Father.

Though the prospect of getting Christmas presents might drive us to selfish ruminations, our culture still casts Christmas as a family holiday. Paul directs our attention to the unique family Jesus came into this world to build—the church. Jesus rescues individuals by his death and resurrection, but he does that work to form his church. The humility he displayed in his incarnation must set the tone for our life together as his people.

Consider crucial differences between Jesus and the angels. It will help us celebrate Christmas and to be the church Jesus deserves.

THE SON OF GOD DESCENDED TO BE THE SON OF MAN

Some people think that humans can become angels after they die. In the movie, "It's a Wonderful Life," fictional angel Clarence does so. It might be a wonderful movie but it features lousy angelology. The Bible teaches that angels are angels, humans are humans, and their natures remain separate.

Most people know angels play a part in the Christmas story. Many have seen children play church pageant angels, sporting aluminum foil halos. To put it mildly, the real nativity angels were more striking.

We read previously about a wild experience had by father-to-be Joseph. Matthew 1:20 reports, "An angel of the Lord appeared to him in a dream and said, 'Joseph son of David, do not be afraid to take Mary home as your wife, because what is conceived in her is from the Holy Spirit.'" Joseph was not a victim of late noshing. He did not pound down pickled herring, chopped liver, and gribenes before bed (Gentiles might have to Google that). He had a divine vision and got a healthy taste of reality.

Luke chapter 2 tells us about an angelic airborne operation the night Jesus was born. An angel of the Lord appeared to shepherds as the pathfinder for the main division that suddenly dropped into those fields. They told good news but their grandeur terrified the shepherds. Angels are grand, but the small boy in the manger was infinitely majestic. His descent topped all.

What happens when angels descend to earth? Creatures that are native to one part of creation move to another part. They make a breathtaking drop, but the whole journey remains within the created order. Their descent is largely a change of scenery. Their experience resembles the descent scuba divers make. Divers use equipment suited to a foreign environment but their nature remains unchanged. God gives visiting angels the special equipment of semi-human appearance but their nature remains unchanged.

What happened when the Son of God descended to earth? The maker and master of creation moved into creation as part of creation (Jn 1:1-18). He came to us from outside of the created order. Jesus is "Emmanuel" which means "God with us." When we sing, "O Come, O Come Emmanuel...descend to us we pray," we celebrate more than a change of scenery for the Son. We honor the Second Person of the Triune God who added a full human nature to his experience.

The Lord's favorite self-description was "the Son of Man." Often Jewish people used "son of" as a figure of speech to point to one's nature. Two of the twelve disciples were originally called "sons of thunder" because of their temper (Mk 3:17). In the Lord's case, the figure of speech indicates that Jesus was a true human. It also marks him as the greatest missional figure ever.

When God the Son became human, he crossed a vast gulf. A greater chasm stands between God and an angel than stands between an angel and a human. No one who knew Jesus doubted that he was human.

But was he still God? Yes. In Colossians 2:9, Paul wrote, "the entire fullness of God's nature dwells bodily in Christ." God cannot stop being God.

God also does not start being God. Note what God declares in Isaiah 43:10-11:

"You are my witnesses"—
this is the LORD'S declaration—
"and my servant whom I have chosen,
so that you may know and believe me

and understand that I am he.
No god was formed before me,
and there will be none after me.
I—I am the LORD.
Besides me, there is no Savior."

God is eternal. This passage rules out any true God coming into being. The Son became a human, but he always was God and always will be. Twice God uses his personal name to declare there is no other Savior.[2] When the Son came to save us, God was on the job personally.

How then do we process Paul's statement that the Son "emptied" himself? Pay close attention to what Paul wrote about the Son in Philippians 2:7: "he emptied himself by assuming the form of a servant." The word rendered "assuming" is the Greek word "lambano" which means to "take." The Son *emptied* himself by *adding.*

The apostle did *not* say that the Son "emptied himself *and took* the form of a servant." That would be a different matter. Suppose I said, "I got wet *taking* a shower." You would know how I got wet: in the act of taking a shower. Suppose I said, "I got wet *and took* a shower." You would not know how I got wet. Maybe I got wet scuba diving in the ocean and then took a shower to rid myself of salt. Maybe I got wet from skunk spray and took a shower. Maybe I got wet by falling into a cesspool and took a shower. Paul told the Philippians that the Son emptied himself *by taking* the form of a servant.

What does "form" mean here? It does not mean a human-like appearance (as with angel visits) because Paul says the Son appeared *as* a man. When I was in grade school, I appeared in a school production playing the part of Charles Lindbergh. I wore snow boots, a scarf, and ski goggles, trying hard *to look the part*. I was cute (my mom's view) but I was not an actual pilot, let alone the first one to fly solo across the Atlantic. When Lindbergh made a public appearance, he was the real deal. He appeared *as* the star aviator.

Angels appear *to look like humans*. The Son of God appeared on earth *as a human*. He bore our likeness because he was like us. Unlike the illusions cast by my flat View-Master reels, Jesus is a 3-D human. He worked, worshipped, ate, drank, slept, cried, and died. He rose again and always will live. He is the real deity in human form.

He emptied himself of his right to enjoy his proper estate in heaven. He added a human nature to his experience. No being ever took such a humbling step down.

THE SON OF GOD DESCENDED TO BE THE SIN-BEARER

We talk about average people becoming heroes by rising to the occasion. Jesus did the opposite—he descended to the occasion. The most glorious Son rescued us by becoming a common citizen.

The Son had to become human because he came to rescue humans. Angels descend as messengers; the Son came as the mess-cleaning Messiah. Getting doused by septic tank sludge is a nightmare. Jesus suffered far worse on the cross. No one ever endured anything as awful.

Imagine how burdensome life in this world was for Jesus even before the crucifixion. Sin repulses the holy angels. Angels sometimes visit earth to execute God's judgments on sinners. Angels who never sinned see sin for what it is.

Like those angels, sin repulses Jesus. Yet he came here for a long residency. Angels come here and leave; the Son came and stayed. He lived decades in our mess.

Angels can take comfort in one another's company on their visits to our warped world. The Bible often shows them arriving in large numbers. Jesus stood alone. He was the only pure human being in the world.

Death had infected everyone else. P. T. Forsyth asked: "How should a man feel who was alive, alone in a world of the dead?"[3] Forsyth calls us to imagine the holy one's solitude:

> His life as Man was a real life, and He was bound to feel the last reality of man's deadness. And He alone *could* feel it. *They* were too dead in sin. Alone He fulfilled the condition of feeling a moral death utterly universal, and therefore dreary, cold, loathsome, to such a soul as His.[4]

Multiply the worst loneliness you ever felt millions of times and you begin to approach his burden.

Angels come to execute God's judgment on sinners; God the Son came to satisfy justice for sinners. He came to take our sin on himself. The sinless Christ made our sin his burden to bear and suffered its consequences.

A true story from World War II provides a glimpse of the nasty work Jesus faced. In Shantung Province (now Shandong), China, Japanese invaders placed all non-combatant westerners in one compound and told them to run the camp themselves. Soon the toilets were clogged. Waste piled higher than the seats. The odor offended all the inmates, even from a distance. Langdon Gilkey was interned in that camp. Brace yourself for his blunt statement about the problem:

> The sole contact the average urban Western man has with human excrement consists of a curious look at what he has produced, a swirl of water, and a refreshing bar of soap. Consequently the thought of wading into a pool of his fellow man's excrement in order to clean up a public john not equipped with flush toilets is inconceivable.[5]

People feared going near the mess and many thought the cleaning job was beneath their dignity, including executives, government officials, and clergy. Then a small group stepped up and stooped to serve all.[6]

That story would never appear on a Christmas card, but it helps us understand Christmas. Jesus came into this world to clean up a mess infinitely worse than the one in those toilets. The toilets overflowed with a product of biology. Warped desires and willful defiance of our creator made our moral mess.

Heaven finds our sin repulsive even from a distance, yet the Son of God stooped to serve. The job was infinitely beneath his dignity. He crossed a divide even greater than that between Creator and creation—he bridged the gap between God and sin. Charles Wesley wrote: "he deigns in flesh to appear, widest extremes to join; to bring our vileness near."[6]

No angel ever stooped so low. None could. Why did the Son do it? Love times two.

The Son loves the Father and delights to do his will. The Son loves sinners. So he came. David Wells calls us to appreciate the Lord's realism and resolve:

Are we to suppose that in the far mists of eternity, when our calling and redemption were only in the mind of God, Christ was unaware of what this would entail? Was he caught by surprise after he became incarnate? Do we ever hear him reproaching the Father for not having told him what this mission of redemption would cost? Of course not! The point about Christ's love is that he *knew*. He knew from the very start. But such is this love, this self-giving, self-sacrificing, self-abasing love that he freely and joyfully gave of himself to do what had to be done, knowing all that was entailed. Indeed, there is no other motive sufficient to account for what he did than this extraordinary love. For only this kind of love would pay the cost which this kind of mission required. He saw that his own self-giving reached a greater end by becoming incarnate than by not so doing. He willingly chose not to enjoy the worship of the angels in a place of utter holiness for an uninterrupted eternity for the gain that redemption would bring.[7]

The Son came to make us godly by his pure, powerful grace.

In Philippians 2, Paul points to the Lord's humble descent to shape the daily behavior of the church. The Son of God chose to add a servant's nature to his experience and become human. How much more should we behave as servants when our nature is human? He became what he *was not* so our behavior can match what *we are*.

Service is the point. Humility is in; selfishness is out. A church congregation must not be consumers of religious goods and services or providers of the same. Never spell service "serve-us."

Jesus humbled himself and therefore God exalted him. Each church should seek the commendation: "That church humbled itself, therefore God lifted them up." Being a humble church is much better than being a happening church. Never be proud of popular church programs or big numbers. Be humble like the church's savior.

Nothing is as pathetic as pooled selfishness. No congregation will be perfect in this world, but we can all battle our inbred and sin-bred arrogance every step from here to glory. We must do it as reasonable worship (Rom 12:1-21).

The Lord deserves our grateful service. Jesus is not the man of our dreams. He is the Son of Man—our savior, our holy model, and our hope.

Thou didst leave Thy throne and Thy kingly crown,
When Thou camest to earth for me;
But in Bethlehem's home was there found no room,
For Thy holy nativity.
O come to my heart, Lord Jesus—
There is room in my heart for Thee!

Heaven's arches rang when the angels sang,
Proclaiming Thy royal degree;
But of lowly birth Thou didst come to earth,
And in great humility.
O come to my heart, Lord Jesus—
There is room in my heart for Thee!

The foxes found rest and the birds their nest,
In the shade of the forest tree;
But Thy couch was the sod, O Thou Son of God,
In the deserts of Galilee.

O come to my heart, Lord Jesus—
There is room in my heart for Thee!

Thou camest, O Lord, with the living word,
That should set Thy people free;
But with mocking scorn and with crown of thorn,
They bore Thee to Calvary.
O come to my heart, Lord Jesus—
There is room in my heart for Thee!

When the heav'ns shall ring and the angels sing,
At Thy coming to victory,
Let Thy voice call me home, saying "Yet there is room—
There is room at My side for thee."
O come to my heart, Lord Jesus—
There is room in my heart for Thee![8]

CANNONBALLS
AND CHRISTMAS BELLS

*"I have told you these things so that in me you may have
peace. You will have suffering in this world. Be courageous!
I have conquered the world."*
John 16:33

Have you ever enjoyed a snowball fight? That pastime was often
my game in the chilly north. None of us, however, has seen the
likes of the snowball warfare that was a regular feature of camp
life in the American Civil War. Many of those fights occurred in
the South among Confederate units. Some were huge. Soldiers
waged a giant melee in Virginia after 17 inches of snow fell over
3 days in February of 1863.

Historian Bell Irvin Wiley notes that soldiers loved building
snowmen, skating, and sledding, but nothing bested snowball
battles for beating boredom:

But of strictly winter sports snowballing was by far the
most pervasive and the most hilarious. Day after day, from
the first arrival of a few inches of snow in November and

December until the melting of the last particles by the spring sun, soldiers were wont to pelt each other unmercifully with tightly packed snowballs. Even officers were not spared. "I knew I would have to be snow balled at some time," wrote Colonel C. Irvine Walker from Dalton, Georgia, in 1864, "for the men did not let off any one in the brigade Except Gen'l M. So I thought it would be best to go down and take part in the fight and be snow balled."[1]

If only all battles were merry.

Those snow-dusted soldiers knew the physical, emotional, social, and spiritual horrors of real war. Do we know how Christmas intersects with those horrors? Three men appear in this scene to help us probe that question.

For many of us, seasonal Christmas makes demands no more daunting than updating Giftster, doing Amazon searches, trying adventurous recipes, and scarfing antacids afterward. The three men we will study—two born 1800 years before the third—faced intense suffering.

THE POET

Henry Wadsworth Longfellow was the most popular poet in America in the 19th Century. He penned the following lines:

I heard the bells on Christmas Day
Their old familiar carols play,
And wild and sweet
The words repeat
Of peace on earth, good-will to men!

And thought how, as the day had come,
The belfries of all Christendom
Had rolled along
The unbroken song
Of peace on earth, good-will to men![2]

The poem is titled, "Christmas Bells." Later set to music, it became the beloved carol, "I Heard the Bells on Christmas Day."

Many people know the lyrics but not their context. Longfellow wrote them during the Civil War. We rarely sing two of the original stanzas which evoke blazing cannons and bereavement:

Then from each black accursed mouth
The cannon thundered in the South,
And with the sound
The carols drowned
Of peace on earth, good-will to men!

It was as if an earthquake rent
The hearth-stones of a continent,

And made forlorn
The households born
Of peace on earth, good-will to men![3]

Which wins out in the end? Cannonballs or Christmas bells? Suffering or songs of hope?

That was a hard question to answer for those who felt the misery of a divided nation. In one of Longfellow's poems, a young soldier is shot to death. The writer imagines the fatal bullet searching out the soldier's mother in his remote hometown:

And I saw in a vision how far and fleet
That fatal bullet went speeding forth,
Till it reached a town in the distant North,
Till it reached a house in a sunny street,
Till it reached a heart that ceased to beat
Without a murmur, without a cry;
And a bell was tolled in that far-off town,
For one who had passed from cross to crown,
And the neighbors wondered that she should die.[4]

Unlike snowballs and sleigh bells, funeral bells normally do not inspire Christmas songs.

A bullet reached Longfellow's son Charles who served in the Union Army. The chunk of lead lodged under Lieutenant Longfellow's shoulder blade and shattered part of his spine. In those national and family circumstances, his father wrote his poem, "Christmas Bells," on Christmas Day, 1864.

That was not the poet's first heart wound that chased away Christmas cheer. Years earlier, his wife's dress caught fire. Henry tried to smother the flames by throwing his arms around her, severely burning his face, arms, and hands. She died the next day on July 11, 1861. Five months later, at Christmas, Longfellow wrote: "How inexpressibly sad are all holidays!"[5] The next Christmas, in 1862, he still suffered deep grief: "'A merry Christmas,' say the children; but that is no more, for me."[6]

Did Longfellow give up on Christmas? Perhaps the conclusion to "Christmas Bells" answers that question:

And in despair I bowed my head;
"There is no peace, on earth", I said;
"For hate is strong,
And mocks the song
Of peace on earth, good-will to men!"

Then pealed the bells more loud and deep:
"God is not dead;
Nor doth He sleep!
The Wrong shall fail,
The Right prevail,
With peace on earth, good-will to men!"[7]

Was that last stanza a heartfelt answer or was the poem art for art's sake? Indications say that Longfellow meant it all.

Yet, Longfellow was a Unitarian who did not believe that Jesus was God the Son incarnate or that the Lord died to satisfy divine justice. He did not denounce Christianity, but neither did he embrace biblical doctrine. He held a romantic, mystic view of Jesus. He did not trust Jesus to make right prevail by his return to judge the earth.

Longfellow sided with the Christmas bells in the face of war and wrote lines that moved Christians, but he missed Christ's real solution to the world's greatest problem. Shift attention now to a man who never heard Christmas bells but who believed fully in Christ.

THE PRIME SINNER

Who would you say was the worst sinner? Probably not the man who wrote more of the New Testament than any other person. But he described himself as the worst.

We know him as the Apostle Paul but he originally went by the name, "Saul of Tarsus." One day, Jesus stopped Saul in his tracks as the man hunted the Lord's followers. Jesus called Saul to his service. Saul had done the most to destroy Christianity at the start of the worldwide gospel mission, thereby justifying the "worst" sinner label he later applied to himself.

Jesus became Paul's treasure, yet Paul's life became a litany of suffering after he came to know Christ (2 Cor 11-12). Toward the end of Paul's life, Rome jailed him for preaching Christ as Lord. Nero used the same title, so the Roman authorities regarded Paul's preaching as an attack on Caesar. Sedition was a capital offense.

While awaiting trial, Paul wrote a letter to a young pastor named Timothy urging him to fight the good fight. That expression was not poetry. Paul's service record was written in scars all over his body. Timothy had seen the marks that published how rough ministry can be.

Paul found the reality of Christmas relevant to his hardships and his sin. In 1 Timothy 4:7, he wrote: "But have nothing to do with pointless and silly myths. Rather, train yourself in godliness." The redeemed realist found hope in Christmas. He sourced his strength in the Lord's incarnation as he explains in 1 Timothy 1:12-19:

> I give thanks to Christ Jesus our Lord who has strengthened me, because he considered me faithful, appointing me to the ministry—even though I was formerly a blasphemer, a persecutor, and an arrogant man. But I received mercy because I acted out of ignorance in unbelief, and the grace of our Lord overflowed, along with the faith and love that are in Christ Jesus. This saying is trustworthy and deserving of full acceptance: 'Christ Jesus came into the world to save sinners'—and I am the worst of them. But I received mercy for this reason, so that in me, the worst of them, Christ Jesus

might demonstrate his extraordinary patience as an example to those who would believe in him for eternal life. Now to the King eternal, immortal, invisible, the only God, be honor and glory forever and ever. Amen. Timothy, my son, I am giving you this instruction in keeping with the prophecies previously made about you, so that by recalling them you may fight the good fight, having faith and a good conscience, which some have rejected and have shipwrecked the faith.

Saul pursued Christians to death, so God made him the prime example of the mission's power and mercy. Paul traveled the world saying—and proving—that Jesus can change any sinner's life. Paul logged 13,000 hard miles doing gospel work.

His letter to Timothy shows that Jesus came to deal with all the sin that has wracked and ruined our world. In Paul's relatively short letter he mentions many examples of disobedience and disorder:

- Lies
- Perjury
- False doctrines
- Blasphemy
- Anger
- Strife
- Violence
- Drunkenness

- Idleness
- Love of money
- Dishonest income
- Family breakdown
- Arrogance
- Suspicion
- Seared consciences
- Busybodies
- Malicious speech
- Gossip
- Slander
- Sexual immorality
- Murder

I did not do all the things on that list, but I did enough to merit hell. To think otherwise means to grossly devalue God's holiness. That is the gravest misstep of all. We come now to Jesus as the third person in this scene.

THE PRINCE OF PEACE

You cannot find Whoville with GPS, but you can plot Bethlehem, Nazareth, and Jerusalem. Residents in those locales rubbed shoulders with the Messiah. Jesus trod ground that bore many military and spiritual battles.

The Grinch, Rudolph, and Frosty distract from our troubles. They provide an emotional safety valve but not a lasting solution. Little reality slips into the television specials. Yes, the Grinch steals, classmates bully Rudolph, and Frosty melts as a metaphor for mortality. But troubles are mostly sanitized and summarily resolved. The worst parts of their television world cannot compare with our troubled world.

Jesus ran head-on into our disorder, pain, and guilt. The Bible accounts do not place a soft Messiah into sentimental scenery. The Lord tangled with worldly trouble of all sorts including familial, economic, medical, political, and spiritual. God the Father did not produce fiction; he sent the Son.

Jesus did not insert himself into a holiday snow globe. God the Son decided to become incarnate in a sinful world. Christmas Bible-style goes well beyond a grumpy Grinch, a few callous reindeer, and a top hat in a puddle.

We long for beauty, which gives rise to snow globes and many other holiday traditions. My family often went to New York City at Christmas. The window scenes in stores along Fifth Avenue captivated us. I wanted to climb into them but did not try. I did not want to visit the Midtown North Police Precinct.

I have walked the streets of Manhattan to a spot where two tall towers once stood. They toppled on September 11, 2001. Coordinated attacks also claimed lives in Washington D.C. and Pennsylvania. Terrorists caused at least $10 billion in damage and murdered 2,977 victims from 90 countries.

Can Christmas stand up to that? Yes.

Christianity is a vast rescue operation. It involves an amazing sacrifice to save people from the worst form of death. It deals head-on with evil, so it is sober realism of the highest order.

In 1 Timothy 1:15, Paul says Christ Jesus came into the world *to* save sinners. He did not say Jesus came *and* saved sinners. The cross was not an afterthought; it was the point of the cradle. If you went to visit a friend in a tall building and got stuck in the elevator, you did not go there *to* get stuck between floors—you went *and* got stuck. The Son of God decided in advance *to* be conceived by a virgin, *to* be born as a human, *to* stay on mission, *to* die for us, and *to* rise again. Love drove him to do all of that *to* save sinners.

When the New York City first responders went to work on September 11, 2001, they knew some of them might pay a steep price for their service. None knew so many would die that day or how they would perish. The Son knew before he left his heavenly home that his rescue work was going to cost his life and he knew the cross awaited. Yet, he came.

The Lord's cross was as real as the one made of metal beams that emerged from the wreckage of the World Trade Center. In a stunning act of self-surrender, Jesus took our guilt and died in our place. The pure man died for the impure, enduring much more than the physical agony of crucifixion. He suffered the pains of hell.

The Lord rose bodily from the dead to show he had power even over the grave. His tomb was not made of gingerbread but was as real as rock. The risen Lord stepped past the stone door more alive than ever. He is done with dying.

The living Lord offers eternal life to all who humbly ask him for the gift. We all need his mercy. Do we think we can stand securely before God bearing our record of sin? If so, we indulge in the ultimate fantasy. Deadly escapism is not the answer. Our sins offend the only living God. Under his holy gaze of judgment, we do not stand a snowball's chance in a Virginia heatwave. But we can stand forever in the righteousness of Christ. He graciously gives his standing to every sinner who asks him for the gift.

That gift does not make life easy. For Paul, it made life harder in many ways ending with martyrdom. In some ways (minor by comparison) becoming a Christian made my life harder. I had to face things I had avoided and needed to become more disciplined. Church ministry made demands on me I am glad I did not see in advance.

The cross was the hardest thing ever but yields the best results. Christ's sacrifice provides entrance into heaven when we die. It also provides power for us to grow godlier in this world. Someday Jesus will replace this world with a new one. No more deadly battles then. His people will bask in resurrection glory.

Perhaps life has battered and bloodied your heart. Maybe the holidays are particularly difficult. A friend told me she was glad I was writing this book because so many hardships have slammed into her around Christmas. She reminded me how we had to cancel church staff Christmas parties more than once due to emergencies. One time we had just put on our coats to leave for the restaurant when I was asked to intercept a church member on her way home. She did not know that flames were engulfing her house. Not merry.

Look beyond the holidays to the holy Lord Jesus. Jesus is Lord over the world. He can handle all problems and shepherd us through all challenges.

At a home Bible study, someone asked about a suffering friend from church. I said, "He is doing well, under the circumstances." The study leader said, "Christians should not be under the circumstances, we should live above them." I confess I wanted to smack him. The Bible shows believers (including Paul) feeling the pressure of hardship, sometimes terribly so. Our calling is not to live *above* hard circumstances but to locate all our circumstances *under* greater circumstances. Jesus rules. Nothing tops that fact.

We can have robust hope because Jesus faced indescribably painful circumstances on the cross. Then the circumstances shifted radically. He rose from the dead and ascended to glory. We can look up to him now and know he is in control even when life batters us down here. We find comfort not in denying pain but in relying on the one who reigns.

Jeremy Treat tells the fortifying truth about Jesus the ascended Lord:

Jesus is never surprised, he's never been in a bind; and whatever you're dealing with right now, he's not worried about it. Jesus is sovereign, which means that nothing in your life is a result of his negligence. He's not just 'sitting around' in heaven; he's sustaining the universe from his throne. That's why the right response to the sovereignty of Jesus is not inactivity, but hope. Biblical hope is not wishful thinking; it's unflinching confidence in God's power to accomplish God's purposes in God's timing.[8]

You do not have to pretend all is right with the world. Christianity tells you not to do that. Christ calls you to be a realist who finds perspective and power in his pain as the core of the divine plan for a new world. The Prince of Peace fought the best fight. His epic battle against sin and death produced the ultimate victory.

Cannonballs wound badly but, in the end, Christmas bells win when they sound for the true Christ. He rules. His kingdom is forever.

All glory to God in the sky,
And peace upon earth be restored!
O Jesus, exalted on high,
Appear our omnipotent Lord!
Who meanly in Bethlehem born,
Didst stoop to redeem a lost race,

Once more to thy creature return,
And reign in thy kingdom of grace.

When thou in our flesh didst appear,
All nature acknowledged thy birth;
Arose the acceptable year,
And Heaven was opened on earth;
Receiving its Lord from above,
The world was united to bless
The Giver of concord and love,
The Prince and the Author of peace.

O wouldst thou again be made known,
Again in thy Spirit descend,
And set up in each of thine own
A kingdom that never shall end!
Thou only art able to bless,
And make the glad nations obey,
And bid the dire enmity cease,
And bow the whole world to thy sway!

Come then to thy servants again,
Who long thy appearing to know;
Thy quiet and peaceable reign
In mercy establish below:
All sorrow before thee shall fly,

And anger and hatred be o'er;
And envy and malice shall die,
And discord afflict us no more.

No horrid alarum of war
Shall break our eternal repose;
No sound of the trumpet is there,
Where Jesus' Spirit o'erflows:
Appeased by the charms of thy grace,
We all shall in amity join,
And kindly each other embrace,
And love with a passion like thine.[9]

SCENE FIVE

CHOCOLATE, CHRISTMAS, AND CHRIST

*"But solid food is for the mature—for those whose senses
have been trained to distinguish between good and evil."*
Hebrews 5:14

It was Christmas Eve but the mood was not merry. In New York City, Santa Claus was on trial. Fear not. I only refer to a movie: "Miracle on 34th Street."

Kris's lawyer argued that Kringle's noggin was not cracked like a holiday walnut. To prove his client's sanity, he read official post office regulations. The prosecutor objected saying, "It hardly has any bearing on this case." Santa's attorney replied, "It has a great deal, your honor, if I may be allowed to proceed."[1] Allow me to proceed, even if my next statements seem odd.

The United States Food and Drug Administration Center for Food Safety and Applied Nutrition publishes regulations about food purity. They explain their role:

Title 21, Code of Federal Regulations, Part 110.110 allows the Food and Drug Administration (FDA) to establish maximum levels of natural or unavoidable defects in foods for human use that present no health hazard. These "Food Defect Action Levels" listed in this booklet are set on this premise—that they pose no inherent hazard to health.... The FDA set these action levels because it is economically impractical to grow, harvest, or process raw products that are totally free of non-hazardous, naturally occurring, unavoidable defects.... The levels represent limits at which FDA will regard the food product "adulterated"; and subject to enforcement action under Section 402(a)(3) of the Food, Drug, and Cosmetics Act.[2]

The FDA acts only if foods exceed stated limits. Here are a few examples of when the government intervenes:

- Cranberry sauce: Average mold count more than 15% volume
- Potato chips: Average of 6% or more pieces by weight contain rot
- Canned tomatoes: Average of 10 or more fly eggs per 500 grams
- Frozen broccoli: Average of 60 or more aphids and/or thrips and/or mites per 100 grams
- Golden Raisins: Average of 40 mg or more of sand and grit per 100 grams; 10 or more whole or equivalent insects and 35 Drosophila eggs per 8 ounces

- Asparagus: 10% by count of spears or pieces are infested with 6 or more attached asparagus beetle eggs and/or sacs
- Mushrooms: Average of over 20 or more maggots of any size per 100 grams of drained mushrooms and proportionate liquid

This list provokes questions. Is there a chip bag that boasts 95% rot free? How cute do those dancing raisins seem now? Are you planning any holiday menu changes?

I find the chocolate regulation most disturbing. The FDA allows up to 60 insect fragments and 2 rodent hairs per 100 grams. A large candy bar can have 120 insect fragments and 2 rodent hairs and still pass FDA inspection on the way to your tummy. Is it too late to take back that Godiva sampler? Be glad I left out action levels for nutmeg and popcorn.

It may seem those gross groceries have hardly any bearing on Christmas, but they have a great deal to do with why Jesus came into the world. I cited the regulations to highlight standards. God has the highest standards. God the Son met all of them here on earth.

The Bible teaches that holiness is central to Christmas. The angel Gabriel told Mary: "The Holy Spirit will come upon you, and the power of the Most High will overshadow you. Therefore, the holy one to be born will be called the Son of God." (Lk 1:35). Jesus is the holy one, but what does the word "holy" mean?

Someone might say to me, "Everyone knows that." But pressed, the person might stammer, "It means... It's kind of like…. Well, doesn't it have something to do with being passionately religious?" Not quite. For example, we sing "O Holy Night" to describe the time Jesus was born, but how can a night be passionate about religion? We must go deeper.

GLORIOUSLY SET APART

The word "holy" means, "set apart." God is holy. He surpasses all supposed competitors. No creature compares.

We should be most deeply impressed with God. Angels are. Psalm 89:7 says: "God is greatly feared in the council of the holy ones, more awe-inspiring than all who surround him." Isaiah 8:13 tells God's chosen people, "You are to regard only the LORD of Armies as holy. Only he should be feared; only he should be held in awe." God is in a class by himself.

Back to Christmas. That Bethlehem night was holy because it was set apart from all other nights. The child born in the manger is the only human ever conceived in a woman's womb by the direct work of God the Holy Spirit. The special child made the night special. That is why we sing lines like, "silent night, holy night." God entered the world as a human only once. It was the grandest entrance of all. The sovereign Lord came for commoners like me. His merciful mission sets him apart from all other benefactors.

TERRIBLY SET APART

Jesus is the best but sin is the worst. How bad is sin? It is so serious that sinners merit eternal separation from God—the worst way to be set apart. Jesus taught the sobering truth of hell (Matt 5:22, 29, 30, 10:28, 18:8-9; 23:15, 33). Then he faced it. He accepted a mission no one else could accomplish. He came for the wrong we have all done.

God sees every sin of every size and every sort. He sees more than robbery, murder, oppression, and genocide. When Isaiah saw God as holy, holy, holy, he thought first of his unclean mouth (Isa 6). Sin pervades our lives more than we think. God sees all greed, envy, gossip, lies, lust, disrespect, brawling, and selfishness. The Lord's Prayer directs us to pray that God's will be done on earth as it is in heaven (Matt 6:10). None of the above wrongs happen on high.

In our culture, sin is a marketing tool. For example, an ice cream shop features, "Triple Chocolate Sin." That shop does not offer, "Triple Strawberry Holiness." Sanctity does not sell. Our culture associates sin with a good time. God pronounces judgment on that absurd evaluation in Isaiah 5:20-21:

> Woe to those who call evil good and good evil, who substitute darkness for light and light for darkness, who substitute bitter for sweet and sweet for bitter. Woe to those who consider themselves wise and judge themselves clever.

We all have been too clever.

God set standards long before the FDA did. He never underestimates or overestimates anything. He says sin is a terrible problem, deadly to body and soul.

Theologian Cornelius Plantinga explains sin's nature: "Sin is the smearing of relationship, the grieving of one's divine parent and benefactor, a betrayal of the partner to whom one is joined by a holy bond."[3] He adds that sin, "is a despoiled nature, a diseased root, a contaminated spring, a foul heart."[4]

If I offered you mushrooms from a 100-gram bowl and told you that 19 maggots were spoiling them, you would probably not eat them, even though the FDA says it is OK to chow down. If you dislike mushrooms, substitute something you prefer contaminated with rot, mold, decomposition, or rodent hair. Would you use the befouled food to create a party platter? Your guests would reject the cuisine—and your next invitation—if they knew that you did.

What do you expect God to accept from you? How much coldness can you serve to your holy creator? How much ingratitude? How much gossip? How much bitterness? How much envy? How much greed? How much deceit? How much lust?

I hate maggots. My stomach is strong but those get to me. One day, our dog discovered a dead rabbit. I picked up the bunny carcass and maggots spilled out. I almost lost my lunch. Stop and think. God made fly larvae and they have their place. God did not make the foul behaviors I cited in the previous paragraph.

They disgust him and have no place in heaven. Our culture may find sin tasty, but sin repulses God.

The FDA headed their food standards list by saying the acceptable defects pose no inherent hazard to our health. They set their action levels higher than we might prefer because they deem it impractical to produce food free of defects. Some might apply that approach to human conduct and say, "Of course, we do not want to endorse obvious wrongs like kidnapping, arson, rape, and the Holocaust. But why not accept that the average person is bound to have naturally occurring, unavoidable defects?"

Acceptance of sin is not the answer; acceptance of the savior is.

Some protest, "But God is love." True. God loves more than we consider. He loves purity, truth, and goodness. People leave those divine loves out of reckoning while making excuses for sin.

God also loves sinners. He loves us, not by minimizing our offenses but by saving us from them. Our sin overstepped God's moral "Defect Action Level," but he took gracious action when he sent the savior. He sent his Son to rescue those who trust in him. The cost to Jesus was enormous.

God did not have to do that. Jesus did not merit death because he never sinned. He willingly took the penalty for our sin on his cross. Underestimate sin, and you undervalue the Savior. Value the savior and you learn to turn from sin by his grace.

An easy-going God is a wish projection. A live-and-let-live, hands-off deity might delight us in theory, but we could not depend on him. The living God is dependable because he has pure, consistent standards. Theologian Harry Blamires wrote a novel in which a character says, "I don't believe in a moralistic God, who's got His head so stuffed up with notions of propriety that He can take notice of nothing but acts of petty thieving and trivial dishonesty. My God is much bigger than that." Another character replies, "Why can't you have a God who is bigger still? Not only the Creator of the dawn but also a Redeemer, personally interested in how you and I behave?"[5] The second one is the real God.

God cares about right and wrong. If he did not, we could not trust him for *anything*. But we must trust him for salvation from sin. Please do.

The gift of life is free but is not ineffective. He changes our lives by his grace. We grow more like him by trusting him daily. If you do not want to change, then you do not want Jesus. But that is a fool's stance. Silly me—I stood that way even while sitting through gospel sermons. I finally faced the facts of sin and salvation on God's terms. I asked him for the gift. Now I gladly accept those once-scary changes.

GLORIOUSLY SATISFIED

I read an article about a chef who made rich, expensive chocolates. At first, he loved gobbling on the job. Then he reached the point where he had eaten too much chocolate.

We will *never* have too much gospel grace and glory.

God has better things planned for us than a never-ending Wonka factory tour. The new heavens and earth will be far greater. Perhaps God will toss in some chocolate and calories will not count. I know one thing: the time will never come when we get sick of the holy one.

He is the source of all the good things you ever enjoyed. "Taste and see that the LORD is good. How happy is the person who takes refuge in him! (Psa 34:8). I like feasts but I love Jesus for what he did for me.

God the Son made time. He made galaxies. He made salvation. There is no one like him. He made us for himself. He knows that he alone can satisfy us. Trust the holy one. Taste and see.

O holy night! The stars are brightly shining,
It is the night of the dear Savior's birth;
Long lay the world in sin and error pining,
Till He appeared and the soul felt its worth.
A thrill of hope the weary world rejoices,
For yonder breaks a new and glorious morn;
Fall on your knees, Oh, hear the angels' voices!
O night divine, O night when Christ was born!
O night, O holy night, O night divine!

Led by the light of faith serenely beaming,
With glowing hearts by His cradle we stand;

So led by the light of a star sweetly gleaming,
Here came the wise men from Orient land.
The King of kings lay thus in lowly manger,
In all our trials born to be our Friend;
He knows our need, To our weakness is no stranger.
Behold your King, before Him lowly bend!
Behold your King, before Him lowly bend!

Truly He taught us to love one another;
His law is love and His gospel is peace;
Chains shall He break, for the slave is our brother,
And in His name all oppression shall cease.
Sweet hymns of joy in grateful chorus raise we,
Let all within us praise His holy name;
Christ is the Lord, Oh, praise His name forever!
His pow'r and glory evermore proclaim!
His pow'r and glory evermore proclaim![6]

A MARY CHRISTMAS

"The God of all grace, who called you to his eternal glory
in Christ, will himself restore, establish, strengthen, and
support you after you have suffered a little while. To him be
dominion forever. Amen."
1 Peter 5:10-11

The Snoopy balloon landed back in storage. Black Friday vacuumed our bank accounts. The disposal digested the turkey scraps. All the signs say that Christmastime is here. Our culture knows the routine. A popular song (in more than 500 editions) sets the goal: "Have yourself a merry little Christmas, let your heart be light; from now on, our troubles will be out of sight."[1]

While our culture settles in for a merry little Christmas, we can do more. We can learn to live well by pondering Mary's Christmas.

Holiday traditions generally keep troubles out of sight. Most Christmas customs are chipper but some exceptions stand out. In Iceland, the Christmas cat eats children who get no new clothes for Christmas. They become cat food because they did not help with the spinning and knitting. That tradition makes gift socks more appealing.

I wish you a merry Christmas, cat free if you prefer. But we do not always get a merry little Christmas. Troubles do not stay out of sight just because the calendar flips to the twelfth month. Because of the gospel, we can have better than a little Christmas. We can build our faith by seeing how Mary faced big challenges.

THE HARDSHIP OF BEING HIGHLY FAVORED

Luke 1:26-38 records how Mary received a unique blessing:

> In the sixth month, the angel Gabriel was sent by God to a town in Galilee called Nazareth, to a virgin engaged to a man named Joseph, of the house of David. The virgin's name was Mary. And the angel came to her and said, "Greetings, favored woman! The Lord is with you." But she was deeply troubled by this statement, wondering what kind of greeting this could be. Then the angel told her, "Do not be afraid, Mary, for you have found favor with God. Now listen: You will conceive and give birth to a son, and you will name him Jesus. He will be great and will be called the Son of the Most High, and the Lord God will give him the throne of his father David. He will reign over the house of Jacob forever, and his kingdom will have no end." Mary asked the angel, "How can this be, since I have not had sexual relations with a man?" The angel replied to her, "The Holy Spirit will come

upon you, and the power of the Most High will overshadow you. Therefore, the holy one to be born will be called the Son of God. And consider your relative Elizabeth—even she has conceived a son in her old age, and this is the sixth month for her who was called childless. For nothing will be impossible with God." "See, I am the Lord's servant," said Mary. "May it happen to me as you have said." Then the angel left her.

She was the only woman in history to become pregnant without the participation of any man in any way. Many people would doubt that fact and Mary had to face them.

She heard the miraculous plan and then..."the angel left her." Have you ever been mistrusted, misrepresented, and maligned? Having an imposing angel around to set the record straight would be handy. The maternity plan for Mary did not provide that benefit.

The poet Rupert Brooke poignantly imagined the angelic departure:

> The great wings were spread
> Showering glory on the fields, and fire
> The whole air, singing, bore him up, and higher,
> Unswerving, unreluctant. Soon he shone
> A gold speck in the gold skies; then was gone
> The air was colder, and grey. She stood alone.[2]

Some people would shun this lonely soul.

The angel left her. God did not. He remained her focus and her strength. So, Mary sang God's praises. Luke 1:46-49 records part of the song:

> And Mary said:
> "My soul magnifies the Lord,
> and my spirit rejoices in God my Savior,
> because he has looked with favor
> on the humble condition of his servant.
> Surely, from now on all generations
> will call me blessed,
> because the Mighty One
> has done great things for me,
> and his name is holy."

People in *all* generations have called Mary blessed, but *not all* people in all generations have said nice things about her. Claims against Mary say she was a fornicator, a liar, and insane. Skeptics of all stripes reject the virgin birth.

Mary did not complain about this double-edged blessing. She proclaimed she was the Lord's servant, ready to fulfill the prophetic word. She was not fooling around. The word for "servant" here literally means "slave."

A HUSBAND'S HARD FEELINGS

We saw earlier how God's messianic plan tossed a wrench into Joseph's marital plan. Matthew 1:18-19 shows Joseph reacting to the pregnancy:

> The birth of Jesus Christ came about this way: After his mother Mary had been engaged to Joseph, it was discovered before they came together that she was pregnant from the Holy Spirit. So her husband, Joseph, being a righteous man, and not wanting to disgrace her publicly, decided to divorce her secretly.

The person closest to Mary thought she was unfaithful. Can you imagine the couple's pain?

A betrothal lasted about a year and was considered a legal marriage. Joseph was Mary's husband even though he had not yet taken her to his home or had physical intimacy with her. Divorce was the usual result when a woman committed adultery. If Joseph proceeded with his plan, Mary would be vulnerable. No respectable man would marry a divorced adulteress.

Joseph deemed Mary an adulteress. It broke his heart and he planned the divorce discreetly for her sake. Did Mary tell Joseph about the angel? We do not know. If she did *not* tell him, she showed remarkable reliance on the Lord. Could you wait for

God to bring Joseph into the loop? If she *did* tell him, Joseph did not believe her. Either way, she stood firm.

In time, God provided angelic corroboration of her faithfulness to Joseph as reported in Matthew 1:20-25:

> But after he had considered these things, an angel of the Lord appeared to him in a dream, saying, "Joseph, son of David, don't be afraid to take Mary as your wife, because what has been conceived in her is from the Holy Spirit. She will give birth to a son, and you are to name him Jesus, because he will save his people from their sins." Now all this took place to fulfill what was spoken by the Lord through the prophet: "See, the virgin will become pregnant and give birth to a son, and they will name him Immanuel," which is translated as "God is with us." When Joseph woke up, he did as the Lord's angel had commanded him. He married her but did not have sexual relations with her until she gave birth to a son. And he named him Jesus.

We have no record of further angelic intervention to assure doubters of Mary's virtue. The couple faced stares, smirks, and cold shoulders. Rather than retreat, they advanced together.

A ROUGH ROAD AND NO ROOM

Luke 2:1-7 provides the reason for the family trip to Bethlehem:

> In those days a decree went out from Caesar Augustus
> that the whole empire should be registered. This first reg-
> istration took place while Quirinius was governing Syria.
> So everyone went to be registered, each to his own town.
> Joseph also went up from the town of Nazareth in Galilee,
> to Judea, to the city of David, which is called Bethlehem,
> because he was of the house and family line of David, to be
> registered along with Mary, who was engaged to him and
> was pregnant. While they were there, the time came for her
> to give birth. Then she gave birth to her firstborn son, and
> she wrapped him tightly in cloth and laid him in a manger,
> because there was no guest room available for them.

The divine plan set the Messiah's birth in King David's native
city. Despite the regal connection, the trip was a royal pain. It
took about a week for average (non-pregnant) folks to complete
the journey. No donkey appears in the Bible accounts. We do
not know how Mary made the trip during advanced pregnancy.
She covered about 90 miles of road which ascended over 1,300
feet to Bethlehem.

The couple safely reached Bethlehem but found no normal
accommodations. Weary travelers dread "no vacancy" signs

under far less trying circumstances. Today some hotels give couples named Mary and Joseph free rooms on Christmas Eve. The chosen Mary delivered her baby near animals and resorted to a feed trough crib.

A BRUTAL BLESSING

The family soon moved on to Jerusalem for a dedication ceremony. Luke 2:25-33 records an amazing encounter:

> There was a man in Jerusalem whose name was Simeon. This man was righteous and devout, looking forward to Israel's consolation, and the Holy Spirit was on him. It had been revealed to him by the Holy Spirit that he would not see death before he saw the Lord's Messiah. Guided by the Spirit, he entered the temple. When the parents brought in the child Jesus to perform for him what was customary under the law, Simeon took him up in his arms, praised God, and said, "Now, Master, you can dismiss your servant in peace, as you promised. For my eyes have seen your salvation. You have prepared it in the presence of all peoples—a light for revelation to the Gentiles and glory to your people Israel. His father and mother were amazed at what was being said about him.

Simeon did not stop there. Luke 2:34-35 tell us that he added a blessing—not one you have heard at a baby dedication:

> Then Simeon blessed them and told his mother Mary, "Indeed, this child is destined to cause the fall and rise of many in Israel and to be a sign that will be opposed—and a sword will pierce your own soul—that the thoughts of many hearts may be revealed."

You could understand if the couple said to Simeon, "With a blessing like that, who needs a curse." They did not. They took the hard words along with the happy ones and raised their son in the faith. Luke 2:41 tells us, "Every year his parents traveled to Jerusalem for the Passover Festival." They went out of their way to worship, making the long trek from Nazareth to Jerusalem.

The sword stroke cut Mary's heart years later. On a hill close to that temple, she watched her son die on a blood-saturated cross. He died a brutal death to bless us.

ON THE ROAD AGAIN AND AGAIN AND AGAIN

They went back to Bethlehem after that dedication ceremony, but not to stay. The wise men visited them and then they hit the road again under duress. Evil King Herod had plans of his own regarding Jesus. Matthew 2:13 tells us that after the wise men left, "an angel of the Lord appeared to Joseph in a dream, saying, 'Get up! Take the child and his mother, flee to Egypt, and stay there until I tell you. For Herod is about to search for the child to kill him.'" They took an alternate road to Egypt to avoid going through Jerusalem. The trip was about 350 miles—roughly four times as long as the one from Nazareth to Bethlehem. God could have struck Herod dead. Instead, he sent Joseph, the highly favored Mary, and Jesus the holy one through a desert, chased by a death warrant.

Reflect on what this tells us about God and trials. God had used angels to execute judgment on people before the angel warned Joseph. Why not dispatch an angel to eliminate Herod? Take that approach and you eliminate the trip to Egypt. It seems obvious to us.

We face two options. Option #1 is to conclude that the New Testament writers were so dull that they did not see the obvious. Why, then, have their writings profoundly influenced intellectual history? Option #1 is an arrogant conclusion.

Option #2 is to conclude that the writers reported the actions of the living God who does not always work as we would. He has the whole plan in mind while we have limited minds. Option #2 is a humble conclusion.

I go with #2. Do you?

Psalm 131 calls believers to trust God in a childlike manner:

LORD, my heart is not proud;
my eyes are not haughty.
I do not get involved with things

too great or too wondrous for me.
Instead, I have calmed and quieted my soul
like a weaned child with its mother;
my soul is like a weaned child.
Israel, put your hope in the LORD,
both now and forever.

It is *childish* to think we can figure out why God allows things like Herod's evil acts. It is *childlike* to trust that God has things in hand. When I was a child, I could not always discern the plan behind my parents' wise actions, but I trusted them. I should give God the same courtesy.

My conscience should tell me not to judge God. I know I have done wrong. I am in no position to judge the holy God. Sin warps our thinking about justice, especially applied to self. Most of us struggle with the problem of evil only when it takes a form we hate. When evil is something we enjoy, we do not struggle. When we sin in pleasurable ways, we don't agonize, "How could a good God allow me to do this?" That question disappears while we cheat on our taxes, watch filth, badmouth people, lust, or lie to make ourselves look good.

We are so inconsistent. We suffer and cry out: "If God is good (meaning kind) why did this happen to me? After all, I am a nice person." When something wonderful happens, we rarely hear: "If God is good (meaning holy) why did this happen to me? After all, I am a sinner."

As saved sinners, we do not have all the answers to the questions raised by evil and suffering. David Wells provides perspective: "Our reconciliation has overcome our broken relationship with the Father but it has not conferred on us vast powers of understanding into his governance of the world."[3] I struggled with high school physics class while others easily grasped the subject. How can I master a subject—properly governing the universe—that only God can ace?

I know one thing: the hurts of this world are all, directly or indirectly, rooted in people turning away from God. Do not compound the problem by turning from God because of hurts. Turn toward the eternal solution in God's saving grace. Christians do not have a syllogism that solves all logical problems; we have the Savior that solves our worst problem. We have the man of sorrows who is now satisfied with resurrection life.

When Jesus came for sinners, God the Father allowed his Son to remain under trials rather than provide the immediate solution we would envision. Will we accept the same treatment God the Father gave the incarnate Son? We should. The incarnate Son took the treatment we earned on his cross to reconcile us to the Father.

Back to the account of the Lord's childhood. Time passed and so did Herod. The Lord's family went home to Nazareth where the angel first told Mary she was greatly blessed.

Dislocation was the name of the game for years. Highly-favored Mary journeyed from Nazareth to Bethlehem, to

Jerusalem, to Bethlehem, to Egypt, and to Nazareth. She remained in the state she adopted at the start—as the bondservant of the Lord.

The culture says, "Have yourself a merry little Christmas." The question is, do we have a Mary mind? Do we gladly deem ourselves to be slaves by grace? Will we accept burdens *from* and *for* the Lord who blesses us?

Many believers answer that question "yes" today. The persecuted church suffers around the world and more than at any time in history. Converts are disowned by family, dispossessed, and face death warrants every day. Martyrs give their all in Saudi Arabia, the Sudan, Afghanistan, the Maldives, China, Vietnam, India, Burma, North Korea, and many more places. Persecuted believers do not have a merry little holiday but they display Mary's servant heart. They rejoice in the Lord despite brutal burdens.

We have every reason to choose the place of sanctified slaves (Rom 6:15-23). Our master has given us eternal life. He has given us examples like Mary and the persecuted church. He has given us the Holy Spirit to transform us.

Probe yourself with questions from Mary's Christmas and beyond:

- How much disturbance will I put up with for the gospel?
- How much of a burden will I bear?
- Am I willing to be misunderstood even by those close to me?

- Will I endure dislocation for Jesus?
- Am I willing to move from my comfort zone so that others may hear and know Christ?
- Am I willing to move from my comfort zone so that other believers grow?
- What am I willing to risk for Jesus?

Andreas Köstenberger and Alexander Stewart laud Mary and urge us to learn from her devotion:

> How have you responded to God's call on your life, whatever it might be? Or have you withdrawn in fear of the uncertainties of the future and settled for a safe form of Christianity that requires little or no faith and entails hardly any risk? That form of Christianity is both rampant and lifeless. What would it look like for you to step out in fearless faith in response to what you know to be God's plan for your life? Consider Mary, a young, vulnerable Jewish girl whose entire future and hope for a normal life were jeopardized by God's plan for her life. Mary did not draw back in order to protect herself and her future. She embraced God's future and desire for her life. What about you?"[4]

The question is for congregations as well as individual believers. Local church behavior should prove that being a slave of God is a blessing, but dissatisfied people leave churches for many weak reasons. Sometimes they hit the road when a church puts faithfulness over comfort and teaches hard truth. People say, "Life is tough all week. I need an uplifting service when I come to church." They forget that Jesus was lifted up because he served.

Mary magnified the Lord by accepting more than happy experiences. God gave her the resources to bear burdens and fulfill her mission. We have different experiences but the same God.

The original version of "Have Yourself a Merry Little Christmas" did not have the line, "Hang a shining star upon the highest bough." Frank Sinatra put that in. He removed the original line which said, "we'll have to muddle through somehow."[5] The Judy Garland movie "Meet Me in St. Louis" featured the song. The story involved dislocation.

It is good to know that saved sinners can do much better than muddle through distrust, dirt, dislocation, and danger. We can Mary through. We can walk humbly with God by his sanctifying grace. The road will be rough at times, but the ground is firm and the destination perfect. He has highly favored us. Serve him wholeheartedly wherever he leads.

Sing praise to God who reigns above,
The God of all creation,
The God of pow'r, the God of love
The God of our salvation.
With healing balm my soul He fills,

And every faithless murmur stills:
To God all praise and glory!

What God's almighty pow'r hath made,
His gracious mercy keepeth,
By morning glow or evening shade,
His watchful eye ne'er sleepeth.
Within the kingdom of his might,
Lo! All is just and all is right:
To God all praise and glory!

The Lord is never far away,
But, through all grief distressing,
An ever present help and stay,
Our peace and joy and blessing.
As with a mother's tender hand,
He leads his own, His chosen band:
To God all praise and glory!

Thus all my toilsome way along,
I sing aloud thy praises,
That men may hear the grateful song,
My voice unwearied raises.
Be joyful in the Lord, my heart!
Both soul and body bear your part:
To God all praise and glory![6]

SCENE SEVEN
THE THREE KINGS

"God my King is from ancient times,
performing saving acts on the earth."
Psalm 74:12

An 1864 Christmas pageant in New York City called for a new song. To fill the need, John Henry Hopkins Jr. penned a classic:

> We three kings of Orient are:
> Bearing gifts we traverse afar—
> Field and fountain, moor and mountain—
> Following yonder star.
> O star of wonder, star of night,
> Star with royal beauty bright,
> Westward leading, still proceeding,
> Guide us to thy perfect light.[1]

It is a beloved Christmas carol. The first three words, however, contain two questionable items.

First, the wise men were probably not kings. They likely served as court advisors.

Second, the Bible never says there were three of them. Some traditions say twelve. The song's number comes from the three kinds of gifts, but the gift categories do not add up to three kings. Maybe seven travelers each carried gold, frankincense, and myrrh.

The "star of royal beauty bright" was a prelude to a royal battle. Christmas is part of a long war between sovereignties. The hostilities commenced centuries before Jesus was born in Bethlehem. Things came to a head when he came.

Instead of speculating on the number of wise men, consider three kings we know exist. We will see their connection to Christmas and our lives all year long.

KING HEROD

King #1 is Herod. His fight against Jesus begins in Matthew 2:18:

> After Jesus was born in Bethlehem of Judea in the days of King Herod, wise men from the east arrived in Jerusalem, saying, "Where is he who has been born king of the Jews? For we saw his star at its rising and have come to worship him." When King Herod heard this, he was deeply disturbed, and all Jerusalem with him. So he assembled all the chief priests and scribes of the people and asked them where

the Messiah would be born. "In Bethlehem of Judea," they told him, "because this is what was written by the prophet: 'And you, Bethlehem, in the land of Judah, are by no means least among the rulers of Judah: Because out of you will come a ruler who will shepherd my people Israel.'" Then Herod secretly summoned the wise men and asked them the exact time the star appeared. He sent them to Bethlehem and said, "Go and search carefully for the child. When you find him, report back to me so that I too can go and worship him."

The first two verses mention two kings: "King Herod" and "the one born king of the Jews." Herod counted one king too many. Two was not company; two was a crowd. He hated competition.

Rome made Herod their client king to rule over Palestine for their benefit. Herod had a shaky start in the power politics of Palestine. Rome proclaimed Herod king of the Jews in 40 B.C. They backed him with their might and he captured Jerusalem three years later. By the time Jesus was born, Herod held office for more than three decades. That amounts to about eight American presidential terms in a row. No number of years was enough for power-mad Herod.

The wise men posed a provocative question: "Where is he who has been born king of the Jews?" News of a rival sovereign threatened all of Jerusalem's power players. Their influence and identity stood at risk. A royal birthright threw sand into the political machine.

We find two groups of long-distance travelers in Matthew 2:9-15:

> After hearing the king, they went on their way. And there it was—the star they had seen at its rising. It led them until it came and stopped above the place where the child was. When they saw the star, they were overwhelmed with joy. Entering the house, they saw the child with Mary his mother, and falling to their knees, they worshiped him. Then they opened their treasures and presented him with gifts: gold, frankincense, and myrrh. And being warned in a dream not to go back to Herod, they returned to their own country by another route. After they were gone, an angel of the Lord appeared to Joseph in a dream, saying, "Get up! Take the child and his mother, flee to Egypt, and stay there until I tell you. For Herod is about to search for the child to kill him." So he got up, took the child and his mother during the night, and escaped to Egypt. He stayed there until Herod's death, so that what was spoken by the Lord through the prophet might be fulfilled: Out of Egypt I called my Son.

The wise men worshipped Jesus as the Jewish Messiah. A Jewish king decided that making war on the Messiah was wiser. Pick up the events in Matthew 2:16-23:

Then Herod, when he realized that he had been outwitted by the wise men, flew into a rage. He gave orders to massacre all the boys in and around Bethlehem who were two years old and under, in keeping with the time he had learned from the wise men. Then what was spoken through Jeremiah the prophet was fulfilled: "A voice was heard in Ramah, weeping, and great mourning, Rachel weeping for her children; and she refused to be consoled, because they are no more." After Herod died, an angel of the Lord appeared in a dream to Joseph in Egypt, saying, "Get up, take the child and his mother, and go to the land of Israel, because those who intended to kill the child are dead." So he got up, took the child and his mother, and entered the land of Israel. But when he heard that Archelaus was ruling over Judea in place of his father Herod, he was afraid to go there. And being warned in a dream, he withdrew to the region of Galilee. Then he went and settled in a town called Nazareth to fulfill what was spoken through the prophets, that he would be called a Nazarene.

Herod used his first-strike capability. He killed baby boys.

This passage challenges our hearts and minds. How could God allow this slaughter? Should we just shift over to atheism and be done with such conundrums?

No. First, atheism faces plenty of puzzles of its own. Second, the murder of those boys does not indicate there is no God.

103

Instead, it shows what happens when people act as though there is no God. Herod did not believe in the God who revealed himself in the Jewish Scriptures even though Herod was Jewish.

Heroes of our faith, like Mary and Joseph, did more than know there is a God. They longed to know the God that is. They did more than seek to use God; they stepped up to be used by God.

They let God stretch their perception of him rather than quit when they found their conception limited. Most of all, they did not permit their emotions to become their god. Their pain was real but did not rule. They hurt but they humbled themselves and followed the living God even in the darkest times. We must follow their example.

Herod plotted his selfish course and he plotted many murders. By the time of the Bethlehem slaughter, he had already executed many Jewish leaders. He murdered many of his family members including his favorite wife and two favorite sons based on a false allegation that they were plotting against him.

Herod pre-planned his funeral to mitigate the fact that people hated the king. He knew his Jewish subjects would not mourn his passing, so he issued an advance directive. He ordered that, at his death, Jewish nobles be executed. His plan to generate mourning at his passing failed when underlings disobeyed the order.

When the wise men arrived at his palace, Herod was a sick, old man. He soon slipped into eternity. Matthew 2:19 says, "After Herod died." All despots die. Pharaoh died. Nero died.

Hitler died. Stalin died. Mao died. Ceaușescu died. Pol Pot died. Idi Amin died. Saddam Hussein died.

What comes after that? Isaiah 14:9-11 portrays a morbid pageant for a fallen despot:

> Sheol below is eager to greet your coming,
>   stirring up the spirits of the departed for you—
> all the rulers of the earth—
> making all the kings of the nations
>   rise from their thrones.
> They all respond to you, saying,
> "You too have become as weak as we are;
>   you have become like us!
> Your splendor has been brought down to Sheol,
>   along with the music of your harps.
> Maggots are spread out under you,
>   and worms cover you."

Jesus asked, "For what does it benefit someone if he gains the whole world, and yet loses or forfeits himself?" (Lk 9:25). Losing an election is peanuts compared to losing your soul. No throne can compensate.

The Lord's birth gave Herod a royal opportunity to repent. Instead, Herod faked worship to promote sin. Herod built a magnificent temple but he was a magnificent fool. He should have humbled himself and made a penitent's trek to the temple to offer the sacrifices that the law prescribed. Instead, he tried to kill the one who came to be the perfect sacrifice and the perpetual king.

KING JESUS

Herod appeared powerful but was weak; Jesus appeared weak but is powerful. Herod killed people to preserve his kingdom; Jesus allowed himself to be killed to establish his kingdom. Herod's kingdom passed away; the Lord's kingdom is forever.

Years after Herod died, a lesser politico named Pilate skeptically probed Jesus. John 18:37 reports:

"You are a king then?" Pilate asked. "You say that I'm a king," Jesus replied. "I was born for this, and I have come into the world for this: to testify to the truth. Everyone who is of the truth listens to my voice."

Herod and Pilate worried more about their sovereignty than their sin problem. So, they turned from the truth.

Pilate sent the King of kings to die between two thieves. Jesus appeared even less regal on the cross than as a baby in an animal feed trough. Luke 23:35-43 sets the scene:

The people stood watching, and even the leaders were scoffing: "He saved others; let him save himself if this is God's

Messiah, the Chosen One!" The soldiers also mocked him. They came offering him sour wine and said, "If you are the king of the Jews, save yourself!" An inscription was above him: THIS IS THE KING OF THE JEWS. Then one of the criminals hanging there began to yell insults at him: "Aren't you the Messiah? Save yourself and us!" But the other answered, rebuking him: "Don't you even fear God, since you are undergoing the same punishment? We are punished justly, because we're getting back what we deserve for the things we did, but this man has done nothing wrong." Then he said, "Jesus, remember me when you come into your kingdom." And he said to him, "Truly I tell you, today you will be with me in paradise."

Imagine how that thief's day ended. Herod and Pilate never saw such splendor in their best days.

After Jesus died, he showed his power by rising from the dead. No other king made that move. He ascended to heaven and will return to earth as supreme sovereign.

That covers two kings so far. Who is next?

KING ME

Each of us has declared: "I am king." Probably none of us have said those three words, but many actions have made our proclamation. We have sinned against His Majesty on high. Each of us has tried to be King Me. We try to chart courses independent of God's will.

Trying to exalt ourselves, we diminish our wisdom, freedom, and joy. To peg the outcome, I borrow a line Billy Preston sang: "I'm not trying to be your highness, 'cause that minus is too low to see."[2] We sinners try to unseat God from his throne and produce a tragic plunge. Refusing to be the Most High's most obedient subjects, we engage in fatal subtraction. That minus makes all kinds of misery.

You do not have to be proclaimed a king by Rome to love your sovereignty. Each of us has clung to our own will, defying God's rightful rule over every part of our lives. Self-sovereignty takes many forms:

- God says, "Respect authority." King Me says, "But I am the authority on all things me and I do not like taking orders."
- God says, "Get rid of bitterness." King Me says, "Bitterness is my best banquet. I have been wronged and I have the royal right to feast as I please."
- God says, "It is better not to vow than to make a vow and not fulfill it." King Me says, "My partner does not fully please me. I am out of here."
- God says, "Do not grumble and complain." King Me says, "Don't make me laugh."

- God says, "Love your neighbor." King Me says, "Life's hard enough. I look out for number one."
- God says, "Hate gossip." King Me says, "That person needs to be taken down a peg and I am happy to do it."
- God says, "Devote yourself to prayer." King Me says, "You have no idea how busy a king can be."
- God says, "Live by my every word." King Me says. "I will let you advise me God, but only when I want your help."
- God says, "I call you to be holy." King Me says, "I deserve to be happy."

What fools we mortals be! We march toward death with heads held high.

Few poems celebrate human arrogance like "Invictus" by William Henley:

Out of the night that covers me,
Black as the Pit from pole to pole,
I thank whatever gods may be
For my unconquerable soul.

In the fell clutch of circumstance,
I have not winced nor cried aloud.
Under the bludgeonings of chance
My head is bloodied but unbowed.

Beyond this place of wrath and tears
Looms but the horror of the shade,
And yet the menace of the years
Finds and shall find me unafraid.

It matters not how straight the gate,
How charged with punishments the scroll,
I am the master of my fate;
I am the captain of my soul.[3]

Wrong. Jesus is the master and commander of souls. The scroll of punishment matters and self-reliant sinners face more than coming shade—they face the gaze of the holy judge of the living and the dead (Acts 10:39-43). You either stand before Jesus in the end as the supreme judge or turn to him now as the only savior. Anyone who trusts him will be forgiven by His Majesty's mercy and called to live under his guidance. No third option exists.

The Bible says God the Father made God the Son Lord (Acts 2:36). That divine coronation is not like a democratic election. We cannot vote. We can try to avoid King Jesus, but we cannot make him go away. His term never ends. Jesus is not stuck in a cradle to serve as an unthreatening Christmas decoration. He rules from the top throne.

Eternal life is an undeserved gift. For that mercy, God deserves our unending praise. Preacher A. W. Tozer pinpoints the core of sin and salvation:

Because man is born a rebel, he is unaware that he is one. His constant assertion of self, as far as he thinks of it at all, appears to him a perfectly normal thing. He is willing to share himself, sometimes even to sacrifice himself for a desired end, but never to dethrone himself. No matter how far down the scale of social acceptance he may slide, he is still in his own eyes a king on a throne, and no one, not even God, can take that throne from him. Sin has many manifestations but its essence is one. A moral being, created to worship before the throne of God, sits on the throne of his own selfhood and from that elevated position declares, 'I AM.' That is sin in its concentrated essence; yet because it is natural it appears to be good. It is only when in the gospel the soul is brought before the face of the Most Holy One without the protective shield of ignorance that the frightful moral incongruity is brought home to the conscience. To save us completely Christ must reverse the bent of our nature; He must plant a new principle within us so that our subsequent conduct will spring out of a desire to promote the honor of God and the good of our fellow men. The old self-sins must die, and the only instrument by which they can be slain is the cross.[4]

Every King Me dies. King Me dies by faith at the foot of the cross or dies forever in hell.

The gospel is all about Jesus and his accomplishments. Jesus did not just preach good news; he *is* the good news. The Bible never offers good advice by which we save ourselves. It only offers good news about how Jesus saves sinners.

I used to think I had to scrape up my goodness to offer up to God. I would have to wait to see if I had done well enough for him to overlook my failures and take me to heaven. That thinking is 180 degrees off course. The Bible says that pure goodness comes down to us from glory. God the Son descended to save us by the gory cross (Phil 2:1-18).

I resisted the good news of salvation by grace alone for years because I enjoyed the illusion of self-sovereignty. Finally, I got real and asked Jesus to save me. I gained a good standing with God that is none of my doing. Paul David Tripp's testimony is mine, too:

> In love, he has worked to dent and deface my glory so that his glory would be my delight. He has plundered my kingdom so that his kingdom would be my joy. And he has crushed my crown under his feet so that I would quest to be a good ambassador and not crave to be a king.[5]

Saving faith vacates self-sovereignty and recognizes God's proper place in mind, heart, and will. We realize that God is God and we are not. We cease being the most supreme court jesters and become reverent subjects of the King of kings. We toss aside our silly attempt at supremacy and learn to give the true ruler his due glory.

After King Me died, my life started to change as the true king worked on me. Jesus changed even the way I messed up. I started sinning less and handled failure differently. The old sovereignty tries to rise like a decomposing ghoul, but I petition *King He* to give *King Me* the royal boot and lead me back to paths of righteousness for his name's sake. Jesus does.

Glory awaits on the horizon, perhaps nearer than we think. Unlike the wise men heading to Bethlehem, we do not travel toward glory; glory travels toward us. We will see greater wonders than the wise men did. We will enjoy the prophet's fulfilled promise: "Your eyes will see the King in his beauty; you will see a vast land." (Isa 33:17).

The Christmas story does not enumerate three wise men, but the story concerns three kings. Only one is supreme. Jesus is King. Do not dispute his sovereignty. Delight in it.

> Hark! The herald angels sing,
> "Glory to the newborn King;
> Peace on earth, and mercy mild,
> God and sinners reconciled!"
> Joyful, all ye nations rise,
> Join the triumph of the skies;
> With th'angelic host proclaim,
> "Christ is born in Bethlehem!"
> Hark! The herald angels sing,
> "Glory to the newborn King."

Christ, by highest heav'n adored;
Christ the everlasting Lord!
Late in time, behold Him come,
Offspring of the virgin's womb:
Veiled in flesh the Godhead see;
Hail th'incarnate Deity,
Pleased as man with men to dwell,
Jesus our Emmanuel.
Hark! The herald angels sing,
"Glory to the newborn King!"

Hail the heav'n born Prince of Peace!
Hail the Sun of Righteousness!
Light and life to all He brings,
Ris'n with healing in His wings.
Mild He lays His glory by,
Born that man no more may die,
Born to raise the sons of earth,
Born to give them second birth.
Hark! The herald angels sing,
"Glory to the newborn King."[6]

HAVING PEACE

"Peace I leave with you. My peace I give to you. I do not give to you as the world gives. Don't let your heart be troubled or fearful."
John 14:27

When I was a child, the most wonderful night of the year was Christmas Eve. The word "peaceful" best captures the mood in our house. Regular lamps went dark. Red and green tree lights ruled the night. We lounged in the soothing glow, listened to music, and talked.

I should not paint too rosy a picture. One year my dad had kissing gouramis. That sounds like he contracted a disease that made him hyper-affectionate, but gouramis lived in his tropical fish tank. The fish kiss as harmless challenging behavior. Normally they share the aquarium peacefully. Not that night.

Contrary to the legend of calm animals on Christmas Eve, one nasty gourami kept tearing chunks from another one's tail. I refused to tolerate the injustice. I netted the aggressor and flushed him down the toilet. That night, he slept with the fishes.

ONE HARD HOLIDAY

Christmas Eve, 2005, was not a happy holiday. Cancer was the reason. That disease rips chunks from your heart and your family. My dad was gone, having passed away from cancer two years earlier. My mom endured an 18-hour surgery for a different form of cancer. The operation ran from 8 a.m. on December 22, to 2 a.m. on December 23. I spent that Christmas Eve in the ICU as she held tenuously to life.

It was quiet. I alone could talk because the doctors had intubated mom. We watched red and green lights but they were diodes showing her vital signs. Those monitor lights replaced our holiday bulbs and beeping replaced music.

That night proved a point: having peace tops merely feeling peaceful. Our family had more peace that tough year than in the early holiday seasons. Why? In those early days, we did not know Jesus. In 2005, we did.

In the early years, we knew *about* Jesus. We played carols about Christ. We did not dispute his saving role but we did not depend on it either. Before my mom's surgery, we believed that such specialized teams existed, but we had not depended on them. We approached Jesus in the same way. We labeled ourselves "Christian" but were really "Us-tian." We relied on our best efforts to overwhelm our worst and to open heaven's door. We did not go to church most Christmases. We did not seek the Lord's will and power for each day's challenges and opportunities. Jesus inhabited our manger, but we did not trust him as master.

HAVING PEACE

As peaceful as we felt in the old days, we lacked objective peace with God. Our sin still stood between us and our creator. We had not accepted the solution to our worst problem. We lacked the peace Jesus alone provides.

Feeling peaceful and being safe and secure do not always align. You can sit on a train and feel at peace as it speeds toward calamity at a washed-out bridge. Our family felt peaceful as we sped toward eternity. We calmly raced toward eternal judgment with unready souls.

We felt at peace, in part, because we grossly underestimated our sins and the justice of God. The aquarium incident proves I lacked perspective. A fish biting another fish provoked my sense of justice but I gave myself a pass on selfishness, lies, lust, and more. Such acts wronged God far more than one gourami wronged another.

In Jeremiah's day, some preachers encouraged people to underestimate sin and promised peace as they did so. In Jeremiah 6:14, the prophet laments: "They have treated my people's brokenness superficially, claiming, 'Peace, peace,' when there is no peace." The people led the leaders to say soothing falsehoods. Isaiah 30:9-10 describes the process:

> They are a rebellious people, deceptive children, children who do not want to listen to the LORD'S instruction. They say to the seers, "Do not see," and to the prophets, "Do not prophesy the truth to us. Tell us flattering things. Prophesy illusions."

The people set the terms. The prophets and seers marketed a message they knew would sell. They sold out.

The lowest point comes in Isaiah 30:11 in which the people tell the prophets: "Get out of the way! Leave the pathway. Rid us of the Holy One of Israel." The market demanded flattery rather than salvation.

Peace is more than an emotion. Peace sometimes is a state of positive relations we can "have" even if we do not feel calm. Romans 5:1 says: "Therefore, since we have been justified by faith, we have peace with God through our Lord Jesus Christ." Possessing the best form of peace comes from being "justified." That word means that God made that guilty sinner right with himself while upholding all holiness. Salvation creates peace as a fact, not just a feeling. Having that peace beats feeling peaceful.

In time, our family (each person on a different day) gained that peace by trusting Jesus. We asked him to save us. We talked to him from the heart. No church ritual played a part. We faced God's word on the matter and forsook self-reliance. We looked to the cross and found peace with God.

Psalm 85:10 says: "Faithful love and truth will join together; righteousness and peace will embrace." Gouramis kiss as a harmless challenge; the psalm presents a huge challenge. How does a loving God receive sinful people to himself without violating his purity? The cross joined God's love and the truth about our sin. That sacrifice made righteousness and peace embrace in perfect harmony.

The prophet Isaiah talked about the Messiah making peace the hard way. Isaiah 53 tells us the plan centuries before it happened. Isaiah 53:1-3 shows God works contrary to our expectations:

> Who has believed what we have heard?
> And to whom has the arm of the LORD been revealed?
> He grew up before him like a young plant
> and like a root out of dry ground.
> He didn't have an impressive form
> or majesty that we should look at him,
> no appearance that we should desire him.
> He was despised and rejected by men,
> a man of suffering who knew what sickness was.
> He was like someone people turned away from;
> he was despised, and we didn't value him.

We would make the Messiah look like Arnold Schwarzenegger or Jason Momoa. Jesus would get no call-back from a Hollywood casting director looking for a conquering hero. We would send a Hercules to slay Herod for making the mothers in Bethlehem weep. Instead, God sent a man who wept at a funeral (Jn 11:1-45) and during his triumphal entry into Jerusalem (Lk 19:28-44).

The mundane-looking Messiah had a high and hard calling. Isaiah 53:4-9 shows that his task sent him to his grave:

> Yet he himself bore our sicknesses,
> and he carried our pains;
> but we in turn regarded him stricken,
> struck down by God, and afflicted.
> But he was pierced because of our rebellion,
> crushed because of our iniquities;
> punishment for our peace was on him,
> and we are healed by his wounds.
> We all went astray like sheep;
> we all have turned to our own way;
> and the LORD has punished him
> for the iniquity of us all.
> He was oppressed and afflicted,
> yet he did not open his mouth.
> Like a lamb led to the slaughter
> and like a sheep silent before her shearers,
> he did not open his mouth.
> He was taken away because of oppression and judgment,
> and who considered his fate?
> For he was cut off from the land of the living;

> he was struck because of my people's rebellion.
> He was assigned a grave with the wicked,
> but he was with a rich man at his death,
> because he had done no violence
> and had not spoken deceitfully.

People did not think much of him but he deeply cared for us.

When all seemed lost, he lived. Isaiah 53:10-12 declares that the risen Lord built a spiritual family from his suffering:

> Yet the LORD was pleased to crush him severely.
> When you make him a guilt offering,
> he will see his seed, he will prolong his days,
> and by his hand, the LORD'S pleasure will be accomplished.
> After his anguish,
> he will see light and be satisfied.
> By his knowledge,
> my righteous servant will justify many,
> and he will carry their iniquities.
> Therefore I will give him the many as a portion,
> and he will receive the mighty as spoil,
> because he willingly submitted to death,
> and was counted among the rebels;
> yet he bore the sin of many
> and interceded for the rebels.

The weeping Messiah will have the last laugh. It will last. His family will rejoice forever.

Answer Isaiah's opening question. Do you believe this report? Do you see that Jesus was pierced for our sins? Do you trust his wounds for your healing?

My mom did. That ICU Christmas Eve did not feel peaceful, but mom had peace with God. Jesus had already healed her soul through his cross. Jesus has great plans for her body, too. The doctors went above and beyond but the surgery failed to save her. In early January 2006, she left us. The good news is that she went to her savior. Someday, Jesus will give her a resurrection body. My dad will have one. My sister and I will, too. God's saving grace is the only reason. It is enough. Trust the Great Physician. His treatment works every time.

HARDSHIPS AND PEACE

The apostle Paul taught how having objective peace with God positions us to handle hard times. Paul wrote about the gift of sturdy hope in Romans 5:1-11:

> Therefore, since we have been justified by faith, we have peace with God through our Lord Jesus Christ. We have also obtained access through him by faith into this grace in which we stand, and we boast in the hope of the glory of God. And

not only that, but we also boast in our afflictions, because we know that affliction produces endurance, endurance produces proven character, and proven character produces hope. This hope will not disappoint us, because God's love has been poured out in our hearts through the Holy Spirit who was given to us. For while we were still helpless, at the right time, Christ died for the ungodly. For rarely will someone die for a just person—though for a good person perhaps someone might even dare to die. But God proves his own love for us in that while we were still sinners, Christ died for us. How much more then, since we have now been justified by his blood, will we be saved through him from wrath. For if, while we were enemies, we were reconciled to God through the death of his Son, then how much more, having been reconciled, will we be saved by his life. And not only that, but we also boast in God through our Lord Jesus Christ, through whom we have now received this reconciliation.

Believers *have received* reconciliation; believers *do not achieve* reconciliation. It is wholly a gift. The Lord alone makes salvation by his pure power and we take the gift by faith alone. Peace does not come by church activity or ritual but by placing yourself at the mercy of the savior. We do not make peace with God; God makes peace for us. We either accept or reject the kindest offer.

Paul received that gift and it gave him perspective on hardship. It provided hope that never dissolved under duress. He talks about the patient eagerness he and other believers gain through the gospel in Romans 8:18-25:

> For I consider that the sufferings of this present time are not worth comparing with the glory that is going to be revealed to us. For the creation eagerly waits with anticipation for God's sons to be revealed. For the creation was subjected to futility—not willingly, but because of him who subjected it—in the hope that the creation itself will also be set free from the bondage to decay into the glorious freedom of God's children. For we know that the whole creation has been groaning together with labor pains until now. Not only that, but we ourselves who have the Spirit as the first-fruits—we also groan within ourselves, eagerly waiting for adoption, the redemption of our bodies. Now in this hope we were saved, but hope that is seen is not hope, because who hopes for what he sees? Now if we hope for what we do not see, we eagerly wait for it with patience.

Paul did not whistle past the graveyard. He relied on the resurrection.

My book is about Christmas and the real world. Which world is more real? The present one mired in the fatal fantasy that we can defy God without dire consequences? Or the world to come that will align perfectly with God's eternal holiness? The answer should be clear.

When you know God has handled your biggest problem, you can trust him to help you handle all your problems. You can also trust him to provide a world of peace someday. It does not make life now a piece of cake, but the bread of life fortifies us for the journey from here to there.

I still have some of the records our family listened to on Christmas Eve long ago. One album has the original version of "Have Yourself a Merry Little Christmas." The pre-Sinatra version sounds a hopeful note but lacks confidence. While it says we all will be together, that prospect is only if the fates allow it. While waiting to see, all we can do is muddle through.

My sister and I do more than muddle through or enjoy a little Christmas. We celebrate a great savior. We have the peace that Jesus made for us. We look forward to glory.

When God is ready, his family will all be together. Fates have nothing to do with it. The Father, Son, and Holy Spirit will make it happen. Count on it.

The gathering is for all who turn to Jesus for forgiveness and new life. Will we see you there?

Good Christian men rejoice,
With heart and soul and voice;
Give ye heed to what we say:
News! News!
Jesus Christ is born today!
Ox and ass before Him bow,

And He is in the manger now,
Christ is born today!
Christ is born today!

Good Christian men, rejoice,
With heart and soul and voice;
Now ye hear of endless bliss:
Joy! Joy!
Jesus Christ was born for this!
He has opened heaven's door,
And man is blessed evermore:
Christ was born for this!
Christ was born for this!

Good Christian men, rejoice,
With heart and soul and voice;
Now ye need not fear the grave:
Peace! Peace!
Jesus Christ was born to save!
Calls you one and calls you all,
To gain His everlasting hall:
Christ was born to save!
Christ was born to save![1]

LOOKING BACK AND AHEAD: REEL TO REAL

"The end of a matter is better than its beginning;
a patient spirit is better than a proud spirit."
Ecclesiastes 7:8

I wanted to do more than view the scene. I longed to live in it.

Moonlight cast a blue glow on the deep blanket of snow. Santa just landed on the roof and his reindeer encircled the chimney. Hefting the toy bag over his shoulder, he prepared to descend from the housetop. That vista enticed me more than any other image on my View-Master reels.

I did not foresee the grander landscape I would enter years later. Best of all, it is real and I will stay there. I entered God's kingdom by God's grace. Paul celebrated the best of status shifts in Colossians 1:9-14:

> For this reason also, since the day we heard this, we haven't stopped praying for you. We are asking that you may be filled with the knowledge of his will in all wisdom and spiritual understanding, so that you may walk worthy of the Lord, fully pleasing to him: bearing fruit in every

good work and growing in the knowledge of God, being strengthened with all power, according to his glorious might, so that you may have great endurance and patience, joyfully giving thanks to the Father, who has enabled you to share in the saints' inheritance in the light. He has rescued us from the domain of darkness and transferred us into the kingdom of the Son he loves. In him we have redemption, the forgiveness of sins.

That story has been mine for half a century as a saved sinner.

I forge ahead through hardships because I was present in the worst scene in history. I did not appear there physically, but my presence there is a spiritual fact. Paul located saved sinners at the most heinous crime scene ever. In Galatians 2:20, he declared:

I have been crucified with Christ, and I no longer live, but Christ lives in me. The life I now live in the body, I live by faith in the Son of God, who loved me and gave himself for me.

Someday, redeemed people will live permanently in a perfect world.

I was there when they crucified my Lord. That solved my sin problem and solidified my hope. I will meet Jesus face-to-face.

I desired Jesus and his kingdom all along but had not realized it. C. S. Lewis probed human longing. His comments about books and music apply as well to my old reels:

> The books or the music in which we thought the beauty was located will betray us if we trust to them; it was not *in* them, it only came *through* them, and what came through them was longing. These things—the beauty, the memory of our own past—are good images of what we really desire; but if they are mistaken for the thing itself, they turn into dumb idols, breaking the hearts of their worshippers. For they are not the thing itself; they are only the scent of a flower we have not found, the echo of a tune we have not heard, news from a country we have never yet visited.[1]

The Lord granted me kingdom citizenship in 1972. His promise guarantees my safe arrival in the new creation and perpetual resident status. I still enjoy a peek at the old View-Master scenes on rare occasions, but Jesus merits my enduring, grateful gaze.

My journey has gone from reel to real. I longed for something magical but found the Messiah. Better stated, he found me. I have known hardships of many kinds. Many have come and gone. By God's grace, hope remains. Thank you, Jesus.

> Praise to the Lord, the Almighty, the King of creation!
> O my soul, praise Him, for He is thy health and salvation!

All ye who hear, now to His temple draw near;
Join me in glad adoration!

Praise to the Lord, who o'er all things so wonderfully reigneth,
Shelters thee under His wings, yes so gently sustaineth!
Hast thou not seen how all thy longings have been,
Granted in what He ordaineth?

Praise to the Lord who doth prosper thy work and defend thee;
Surely His goodness and mercy here daily attend thee.
Ponder anew what the Almighty can do,
If with His love He befriend thee.

Praise to the Lord! O let all that is in me adore Him!
All that hath life and breath, come now with praises before Him.
Let the Amen sound from His people again:
Gladly for aye we adore Him.[2]

MY THANKS

My advance readers have encouraged me, snagged many typos in the draft, and suggested valuable improvements. Heartfelt thanks go to the team: David Bush, Evelyn Bush, Natalie Bush, Francine Lawler, Jonathan Lawler, Carol Megaro, Ellen Schmidt, Sean Twohig, Becky Ward, and Christine Yalanis.

Jacey Lawler handled various technical matters.

Jonathan Lawler tracked down elusive sources.

I am grateful to Beth Morgan for all she taught me about writing.

Jess Rainer rose to the occasion for the fourth time. His design team again put my book into an attractive package.

I claim the remaining flaws despite all the help I received.

I thank my family who makes Christmas delightful.

Above all, I praise God the Father for his amazing salvation plan, God the Son for accomplishing it at immeasurable cost, and God the Holy Spirit for graciously applying it to stubborn sinners. Soli Deo Gloria.

NOTES

Preview

1. Anonymous, "O Come, O Come, Emmanuel," trans. John M. Neale and Henry S. Coffin, in *The Hymnal for Worship & Celebration* (Waco: Word, 1986), #123.

Scene One

1. Isaac Watts, "Shepherds Rejoice, Lift Up Your Eyes," in *A Collection of Hymns, for the Use of the Methodist Episcopal Church* (New York: G. Lane & P. P. Sanford, 1842), #488.

2. Abraham Lincoln, *The Life and Writings of Abraham Lincoln*, ed. Philip Van Doren Stern (New York: The Modern Library, 2000), 843.

3. Richard John Neuhaus, *Freedom for Ministry* (Grand Rapids: Eerdmans, 1979), 145.

4. Phillips Brooks, "O Little Town of Bethlehem," in *The Hymnal for Worship & Celebration* (Waco: Word, 1986), #141.

Scene Two

1. David Adler, "The Best No Hitter Follow-Ups in History," Major League Baseball, June 15, 2022, https://perma.cc/UV3E-A9YV; Sam Greenspan, "11 Major League Baseball Feats That Have Only Happened Once," 11 Points, last modified February 24, 2018, https://perma.cc/8TD8-CEHL; Matt Rappa, "Phillies: Story of Richie Ashburn, Baseball's Unlukiest Fan," Fansided (thatballsouttahere.com), accessed August 17, 2022, https://perma.cc/DQ6S-KH35.

2. Michael Brooks, *13 Things that Don't Make Sense: The Most Baffling Scientific Mysteries of Our Time* (New York: Vintage, 2008), 122-135.

3. John Walton, "The Origin of Life: Scientists Play Dice," in *Should Christians Embrace Evolution?: Biblical and Scientific Responses*, ed. Norman C. Nevin (Phillipsburg: P&R, 2009), 195.

4. Nellie Winslow Simmons-Randall, "If You Could See Your Ancestors," tmgenealogy.com, June 13, 2013, https://perma.cc/NU5T-9Y37.

5. Charles Wesley, "Come, Thou Long-Expected Jesus," in *The Hymnal for Worship & Celebration* (Waco: Word, 1986), #124.

Scene Three

1. "At the Circus," American Film Institute Catalog, accessed August 17, 2022, https://perma.cc/5E3Y-CGT2.

2. English versions commonly render the personal name that belongs to God alone as "LORD" and use "Lord" to indicate a leadership title shared by humans. The Hebrew text has only consonants. Because Jewish people stopped pronouncing the holy name, no one is sure what vowels were originally spoken. Scholars favor "Yahweh" as the most likely form.

3. P. T. Forsyth, "The Taste of Death and the Life of Grace," in *God the Holy Father* (London: Independent Press, 1945), 56.

4. Forsyth, 57.

5. Landon Gilkey, *Shantung Compound: The Story of Men and Women Under Pressure* (New York: Harper One, 1975), 14.

6. Charles Wesley, "Let Earth and Heaven Combine," in *A Collection of Hymns for Public, Social, and Domestic Worship* (Charleston: John Early, 1847), #97.

7. David F. Wells, *God in the Whirlwind: How the Holy-Love of God Reorients Our World* (Wheaton: Crossway, 2014), 93-94.

8. Emily E. S. Elliott, "Thou Didst Leave Thy Throne," in *The Hymnal for Worship & Celebration* (Waco: Word, 1986), #127.

Scene Four

1. Bell Irvin Wiley, *The Life of Johnny Reb: The Common Soldier of the Confederacy* (Baton Rouge: Louisiana State University Press, 1987), 63.

2. Henry Wadsworth Longfellow, in *Life of Henry Wadsworth Longfellow: With Extracts from His Journals and Correspondence*, vol. II, ed. Samuel Longfellow (Boston: Ticknor, 1886), 371.

3. Longfellow, 389.

4. Henry Wadsworth Longfellow, "Killed at a Ford," in *The Columbia Book of Civil War Poetry,* ed. Richard Marius (New York: Columbia University Press, 1994), 7.

5. Henry Wadsworth Longfellow, "Christmas Bells," in *The Poetical Works of Henry Wadsworth Longfellow* (London: Oxford University Press, 1908), 534.

6. Longfellow, 534.

7. Longfellow, 534.

8. Jeremy Treat, "At the Right Hand: Why Jesus Being Seated in Heaven Changes Everything on Earth," *Modern Reformation*, vol. 25, no. 3 (May–June 2016): 39.

9. Charles Wesley, "All Glory to God in the Sky," in *A Collection of Hymns, for the Use of the Methodist Episcopal Church* (New York: G. Lane & P. P. Sanford, 1842), #485.

Scene Five

1. Miracle on 34th Street," Internet Movie Database, accessed October 1, 2022, https://perma.cc/J22Z-XW7N.

2. "Food Defect Levels Handbook," U.S. Food & Drug Administration, last modified September 7, 2018, https://perma.cc/4TA8-N56L.

3. Cornelius Plantinga, *Not the Way It's Supposed to Be: A Breviary of Sin* (Grand Rapids: Eerdmans, 1995), 12.

4. Plantinga, 33.

5. Harry Blamires, *Cold War in Hell* (London: Longmans, 1955), 47.

6. John S. Dwight, "O Holy Night!," in *The Hymnal for Worship & Celebration* (Waco: Word, 1986), #148.

Scene Six

1. Maddy Shaw Roberts, "The Original Lyrics to 'Have Yourself a Merry Little Christmas' Weren't Very Merry at All," Classic FM, last modified December 14, 2020, https://perma.cc/C5V6-U7P2.

2. Rupert Brooke, "Mary and Gabriel," in *Chapters into Verse: Poetry in English Inspired by the Bible*, vol. 2 (Oxford: Oxford University Press, 1993), 17.

3. David F. Wells, *Above All Earthly Pow'rs: Christ in a*

Postmodern World (Grand Rapids: Eerdmans, 2005), 261.

4. Andreas J. Kostenberger & Alexander E. Stewart, *The First Days of Jesus: The Story of the Incarnation* (Wheaton: Crossway, 2015), 108.

5. Martin Chilton, "'Have Yourself A Merry Little Christmas': A Classic Christmas Song," Udiscovermusic, December 19, 2021, https://perma.cc/LV7Q-MXBK.

6. Johann J. Schutz, "Sing Praise to God Who Reigns Above," in *The Hymnal for Worship & Celebration* (Waco: Word, 1986), #6.

Scene Seven

1. John H. Hopkins, Jr., "We Three Kings," in *The Hymnal for Worship & Celebration* (Waco: Word, 1986), #166.

2. Billy Preston and Bruce Fisher, "Nothing from Nothing," A&M Records, track 2 on *The Kids and Me,* 1974, record.

3. William Ernest Henley, "Invictus" in *A Treasury of the Familiar*, ed. Ralph L. Woods (New York: Macmillan, 1942), 97.

4. A. W. Tozer, *The Knowledge of the Holy* (New York: Harper & Row, 1961), 36-37.

5. Paul David Tripp, *Dangerous Calling: Confronting the Unique Challenges of Pastoral Ministry* (Wheaton: Crossway, 2012), 181.

6. Charles Wesley, "Hark! The Herald Angels Sing," in *The Hymnal for Worship & Celebration* (Waco: Word, 1986), #133.

Scene Eight

1. Anonymous, "Good Christian Men Rejoice," trans. John M. Neale, in *The Hymnal for Worship & Celebration* (Waco: Word, 1986), #151.

Looking Back and Ahead

1. C. S. Lewis, "The Weight of Glory," in *The Weight of Glory and Other Addresses* (Eerdmans, 1949), 4-5.
2. Joachim Neander, "Praise to the Lord, the Almighty," trans. Catherine Winkworth, in *The Hymnal for Worship & Celebration* (Waco: Word, 1986), #8.

ALSO BY THE AUTHOR

The Corporate Prayer Challenge:
30 Days to Kickstart the Change We Need

Talking Social Justice:
Stories and Questions for Worried,
Wistful, and Woke Evangelicals

A Trail Guide for Church Ministry:
A Proverbial Journey

Available through Amazon